The Bells are Ringing

A CALL TO TABLE

MISSION
San Juan Capistrano

The Bells are Ringing
A CALL TO TABLE

A COLLECTION OF RECIPES
CELEBRATING MISSION SAN JUAN CAPISTRANO

The Bells are Ringing
A CALL TO TABLE

A COLLECTION OF RECIPES CELEBRATING
MISSION SAN JUAN CAPISTRANO

Published by Mission San Juan Capistrano Women's Guild

Copyright © 2007 by
Mission San Juan Capistrano
26801 Ortega Highway
San Juan Capistrano, CA 92675
1-949-234-1300

Photography © by Jon Edwards
Food Styling by Norman Stewart

COVER ART: *Capistrano Mission* by George Brandriff; private collection, courtesy of the Irvine Museum.
Page 198 is an extension of the copyright page.

"When the Swallows Come Back to Capistrano" reprinted by permission of Leon René Publications, Los Angeles, CA.

The proceeds from the sale of this cookbook benefit the preservation of historic Mission San Juan Capistrano.

This cookbook is a collection of favorite recipes, which are not necessarily original recipes.

Mission San Juan Capistrano receives no funding from any religious or government entity
and relies on donations to support preservation.

Library of Congress Catalog Number: 2006900978
ISBN: 978-0-97771-770-5
Tax I.D. 95-1904079

Edited, Designed, and Manufactured by
Favorite Recipes® Press
An imprint of

FRP™

P. O. Box 305142
Nashville, Tennessee 37230
800-358-0560

Art Director: Steve Newman
Book Design: Brad Whitfield and Susan Breining
Project Editor: Linda A. Jones

Manufactured in China
First Printing: 2007   5,000 copies
Second Printing: 2007   5,000 copies

About the Photographer

JON EDWARDS

Jon Edwards has been a professional photographer for well over twenty-five years. Jon's number one claim to fame would have to be the consistent volume of quality work produced from his studio, located in Monrovia, California, as well as on location. He has the ability to juggle the busiest corporate or designer's schedule, fit within any budget and produce the highest quality images, whether they be the latest in digital imaging or conventional film.

A partial list of his clients includes—Earthlink, Vons/Safeway, Palm Springs Life, Contessa, Trader Joe's, Panda Express, Biola University, Meguiar's, BIGHORN, Pepsi, Bristol Farms, Farmer John, Fleetwood, Roland Digital, Pechanga Entertainment Center, Smart & Final, WesCorp, Whole Foods, John Daly, and Kevin Costner, among many others.

While many photographers would have one book to showcase their specialty, Jon would need several—Food, Architecture, Autos, Product, Jewelry, High Tech, and People.

Diana Henderson, associate photographer and digital expert, has worked with Jon for over two years, keeping the studio current with all the latest trends. Diana graduated first in her class from Brooks Institute of Photography in Santa Barbara.

Jon Edwards Photography can be reached at 626-301-9268 or found on the Web at www.jonedwardsphoto.com.

About the Food Stylist

NORMAN STEWART

Norman Stewart, European-trained chef and food stylist, resides in California. He has traveled the globe experiencing different cultures and their cuisines and, to date, has created food designs for twenty-seven varied cookbooks. He is passionate about his work and brings to every project a world of experience and a special touch that makes all of his designs fresh and new.

In the world of commercial advertising, Norman has made his mark. From the beginning, he put his creative genius to work on the "Got Milk?" Moustache Print Campaign, with Lauren Bacall, Elton John and Mohammed Ali, among others. His commercial art can be experienced in such magazines as *Bon Appétit, Food* and *Wine, Vanity Fair* and *Australian Vogue*.

The Mission San Juan Capistrano Women's Guild is most grateful to Norman and his partner, Huggo Brunschkewits, for their contributions to our book. It was, indeed, a pleasure to work with both of them. Norman's assistant Huggo, worked behind the scenes with Guild members and, as a team, all were inspired by the Mission's beauty and spirit.

Contents

Foreword

The California table always had room for another person—whether it was in an eighteenth-century mission, a nineteenth-century ranch house, or a twentieth-century farm kitchen. Travelers could generally find congenial hosts and a basic meal as they ventured from place to place. Accounts of generous hospitality are chronicled in diaries, journals, and letters throughout California's history. The types of dishes served were often described, and recipes sometimes shared. Some of these have remained in families for generations.

The Bells are Ringing—A Call to Table is a wonderful collection of recipes that celebrate the Mission and its rich history. Many are from Capistrano's oldest families; others are favorites with origins in other cultures. In addition to dishes representing the various courses in a meal, there is a wealth of vignettes about the Mission's history, from its founding to the present day. One can feast on the colorful stories of the past while preparing the morning, noon, or evening meal, and all the while be transported back to a time when the pace was slower, food was savored, and mealtime was part of a grand tradition.

Pamela Hallan-Gibson
San Juan Capistrano Historian and Author

Preface

Dear Reader,

Mission San Juan Capistrano Women's Guild was founded in March 1993. Our goal is to assist in the preservation of the historical and cultural heritage of the Mission and promote the landmark for future generations by fund-raising and volunteering for special activities at the Mission.

Our primary focus for the past two years has been the publication of this custom cookbook, which, in addition to delicious recipes, features delightful tidbits of the history and culture of the Mission. Through sales of this book we see a continuous and reliable source of funds for Mission preservation for years to come.

Our members have donated and participated in all manner of fund-raisers. They have tirelessly baked and cooked, researched, and tested recipes. Now all our labors have borne fruit and our book is finally here.

We thank each and every one who purchases this wonderful cookbook. Our hope is that every time you open this book to cook or just to browse, you will think fondly of Mission San Juan Capistrano and know that you have participated in helping to preserve it for future generations to enjoy.

Gracias, Amigos,

The Membership of the Mission San Juan Capistrano Women's Guild

Mission San Juan Capistrano

2006 WOMEN'S GUILD MEMBERSHIP LIST

Roberta M. Amado	Aida Duarte	Anna La Barbera	Lucinda Sire
Ann Allison	Beverly G. Ducey	Maria Lojacona	Mary Smith
Peggy Beal	Lois Eisenberg	Carol Lowe	Jean Spizzirri
Elaine Biegel	Barbara Feiberg	Celia Marquez	Tony Sullivan
Mitzi Birdsell	Denise Finch	Marie McConell	Sheena Sykes
Rose Borgenight	Dorothy Gaffney	Eileen Milroy	Carmen Szladowski
Blanche Brooks	Iris E. Herman	Kim Otamaa	Jessie Talmo
Pat Buchheim	Josephine Hicks	Eileen C. Perkett	Karen Thornton
Joella D. Bury	Mary Jane Higgins	Nina E. Pirkl	Lana Treuhaft
Lee Buser	Judith Hoon	Johni Pittenger	Esmeralda Troge
Joyleen Calef	Joy Horsch	Karen Pollick	Wilma (Willy) Turner
Ruth Casper	Shirley B. Howard	Gloria Ravera	Rhea E. Vogt, Ph.D.
Charmaine Chovil	Beverly Hughes	Beatrice Reyes	Laurie Wilfert
Carol Clisby	Marcia Imonti	Dolores Rosenberg	
Patricia Cole	Deirdre J. Irlam	Pamela Schuler	
Rhoda Davies	Annabelle Isky	Hazel Schwab	
Ann Delaney	Fabiola G. Johns	Linda Schwartz	
Margaret (Peggie) Devlin	Mary Elizabeth Kaiser	Renee Sarafine	*The listing reflects the membership as of March 2006. Any errors or omissions are regretted.
Diana Doll	Angelina Karlson	Dora Simes	

The Bells are Ringing
A CALL TO TABLE

11

Introduction

The Mission San Juan Capistrano Women's Guild cookbook is a product of inspiration and hard work. In fact, when the Guild's leadership first presented the concept of developing a Mission cookbook there were concerns that the product could become a "typical" nonprofit spiral cone bound cookbook. However, the Guild's tenacious leaders, Joy Horsch and Mary Smith, along with their dedicated Board, quickly put my mind at ease as they shared their vision for creating a beautiful, and historically minded cookbook. The Guild understood the importance of having the book represent the Mission as a place of continuing inspiration, education, and preservation. Not only that, but the Guild truly wanted to create a long-lasting source of revenue to support the Mission's preservation, and in their vision was the goal of future publications! After two years of hard work, including recipe gathering, recipe testing, bake sales, fund-raising, and decision making, the Women's Guild has successfully, and beautifully, produced a cookbook for every kitchen.

Food is essential to our experience as humans, and the rituals of shared dining and celebration connect us. As Executive Director, I hope you will enjoy this book, and ultimately, experience a meal that is based upon the Franciscan hospitality of the Mission's tradition. That hospitality continues today by way of *A Call to Table*, and all of us that serve, work, or volunteer on behalf of the Mission congratulate the Women's Guild for their outstanding effort to raise awareness, and funds, to benefit the preservation of Mission San Juan Capistrano, The Jewel of the Missions.

Sincerely,

Mechelle Lawrence
Executive Director

The Bells are Ringing
A CALL TO TABLE

A Call to Breakfast

The Start of a New Day

The Mission buildings form a quadrangle around an open patio which is today called the Central Courtyard. In the early days the patio was alive with the activities of Mission communal life. The grinding of corn and other kitchen chores were done under the shade of the arches which surrounded the patio. The Mission gardens, located just outside the complex, provided fruit, olives, vegetables, herbs, and grain crops. Beyond the complex were open grazing lands for Mission livestock.

Today, the hectic sounds of daily living have been replaced by beautiful and quiet gardens, koi-filled fountains, and the sounds of visiting fourth graders, pilgrims, and visitors from all over the world. However, if you linger long enough in the solitude of these quiet, shaded archways, you might just be able to imagine the tempo of the life that went before.

Our cookbook begins with "Breakfast," the meal that starts the day. Included in this section you will find some historical sketches from The Mission Period, the earliest period of the history of Mission San Juan Capistrano (from its founding in 1776 to Mexican independence from Spain in 1821).

Breakfast Braid

Bread

    2 envelopes dry yeast

    1/2 cup warm water

    1 cup raisins

    1 cup chopped walnuts or pecans

    2 tablespoons all-purpose flour

    2 cups milk

    1/2 cup (1 stick) butter

    1 cup sugar

    $1^1/_2$ teaspoons salt

    2 eggs

    8 to 9 cups all-purpose flour, sifted

    1 egg, beaten

    1 tablespoon milk

Confectioners' Sugar Glaze

    1 cup sifted confectioners' sugar

    2 tablespoons milk

For the bread, sprinkle the yeast over the warm water in a large mixing bowl. Toss the raisins and walnuts with 2 tablespoons flour. Scald the milk in a saucepan. Add the butter, sugar and salt and mix well; cool to lukewarm. Stir into the yeast mixture. Beat in two eggs one at a time. Add enough of the sifted flour to make a soft sponge and beat until smooth. Add the floured raisins and walnuts and enough of the remaining flour to make a smooth dough, kneading until elastic.

Cover the bowl with waxed paper or a kitchen towel and let rise in a warm place until doubled in bulk. Knead again and let rise again until light. Roll the dough on a floured surface and cut into six strips. Make two loaves by braiding three strips together. Place the loaves on a baking sheet and brush the tops with a mixture of the beaten egg and 1 tablespoon milk. Let rise until light. Preheat the oven to 350 degrees. Bake the loaves for 30 to 35 minutes or until golden brown.

For the glaze, mix the confectioners' sugar with the milk in a bowl. Spread over the loaves.

Makes 2 loaves

Czechoslovakian Fruit Rolls

1 envelope dry yeast
1/4 cup warm water
4 cups all-purpose flour
1 cup (2 sticks) butter, softened
3 tablespoons sugar

1 teaspoon salt
4 egg yolks
1 cup milk, scalded and cooled
2 (12-ounce) cans fruit pie and
  pastry filling

Dissolve the yeast in the warm water in a bowl. Mix the flour, butter, sugar and salt in a large bowl. Whisk the egg yolks and milk together in a small bowl. Stir in the yeast mixture. Add the liquid ingredients to the flour mixture and knead for 2 to 3 minutes. Cover with a cloth and chill in the refrigerator for 1 to 12 hours.

Preheat the oven to 350 degrees. Divide the dough into four portions. Roll one portion at a time into a rectangle on a floured surface. Spread 1/2 can of the pastry filling down the center of each rectangle and fold the sides over to enclose the filling. Place two pastries on each of two baking parchment-lined baking sheets. Bake for 30 to 40 minutes or until light brown. Frost with confectioners' sugar frosting or sprinkle with additional sugar, if desired. Cut each roll into eight 2-inch pieces.

Makes 4 fruit rolls

Mission San Juan Capistrano by Alexander Harmer (1886)

Father Serra/Founding of the Mission

The Mission San Juan Capistrano was founded by a Spanish Franciscan padre, Father Juniperro Serro, in 1776. It was the seventh among the twenty-one missions founded in California, and Southern California is privileged to have this important historic site in its own backyard. This "jewel" is Orange County's premier historic site and only mission. Over time, a unique community has grown from the original mission settlement established so long ago. We have endeavored through this collection of recipes and historical notes to provide an idea of the community that is "The Mission."

The Bells are Ringing
A CALL TO TABLE

Acorns Aplenty

Acorns were a staple food of the Acjachemen (pronounced A-ha-sha-men) Indians of the area, and preparing them was labor intensive. The acorns had to be gathered, hulled, pulverized, washed, leached, and then dried. The resulting meal was then mixed with water to form a gruel.

A slice of Applesauce Nut Bread straight from the oven, along with a cup of coffee, is an easier and tastier way to start the day!

Applesauce Nut Bread

Pecan Topping

1/4 cup packed brown sugar

1/2 teaspoon ground cinnamon

1/4 cup chopped pecans

Bread

1 cup applesauce

1 cup sugar

1/2 cup vegetable oil

2 eggs

3 tablespoons milk

2 cups sifted all-purpose flour

1 teaspoon baking soda

1/2 teaspoon baking powder

1/2 teaspoon ground cinnamon

1/4 teaspoon grated nutmeg

1/4 teaspoon salt

1/4 cup chopped pecans

For the topping, mix the brown sugar, cinnamon and pecans in a bowl and set aside.

For the bread, preheat the oven to 350 degrees. Mix the applesauce, sugar, oil, eggs and milk in a bowl. Add the flour, baking soda, baking powder, cinnamon, nutmeg and salt and mix well. Stir in the pecans. Spread in one large or two small greased and floured loaf pans.

Sprinkle the topping over the batter. Bake for 30 minutes and cover loosely with foil to prevent overbrowning. Bake for 15 to 30 minutes longer or until the bread tests done. Cool in the pan for several minutes and remove to a wire rack to cool completely.

Serves 8 to 10

The Bells are Ringing

A CALL TO TABLE

18

Cranberry Bread

2 cups all-purpose flour

1/2 cup packed brown sugar

2 teaspoons baking powder

1/4 teaspoon salt

3/4 cup cranberry-apple juice

1/4 cup vegetable oil

1 egg, lightly beaten

1 teaspoon vanilla extract

1 teaspoon grated orange zest (optional)

1 cup coarsely chopped fresh cranberries

1/2 cup chopped walnuts

Preheat the oven to 350 degrees. Mix the flour, brown sugar, baking powder and salt in a large bowl. Add the juice, oil, egg, vanilla and orange zest and mix well. Fold in the cranberries and walnuts.

Spoon the batter into one greased 4×8-inch loaf pan or two smaller loaf pans. Bake for 55 to 60 minutes or until the loaf tests done. Cool in the pan for several minutes and remove to a wire rack to cool completely.

Serves 10

California Orange Date Bread

1 large orange

1 tablespoon shortening

2 cups all-purpose flour

1 teaspoon each baking soda and baking powder

1/2 teaspoon salt

1 cup pitted dates

3/4 cup sugar

1 teaspoon vanilla extract

1 egg, lightly beaten

1/2 cup chopped nuts

Preheat the oven to 350 degrees. Cut the orange into halves and squeeze the juice into a 1-cup measure. Reserve the orange rind. Add enough boiling water to the juice to measure 1 cup. Stir in the shortening until melted. Sift the flour, baking soda, baking powder and salt together. Pulse the reserved orange rind in a food processor until finely chopped. Add the dates and process until coarsely chopped. Do not over process. Spoon into a large mixing bowl. Add the orange juice mixture, sugar, vanilla and egg and mix well. Add the flour mixture and mix until blended. Stir in the nuts. Pour into a 5×9-inch loaf pan. Bake for 40 to 50 minutes or until the loaf tests done.

Makes 1 loaf

The Bells are Ringing
A CALL TO TABLE

Adobe Brick Structure

The ingredients for adobe bricks are large quantities of mud; cactus juice to serve as a hardener; and binders such as straw, grass, stones, or cow's blood.

To make the bricks, the ingredients are mixed together with a large stick and packed into two- to four-foot rectangular molds. The bricks are baked or allowed to dry in the sun, turning them daily to avoid cracking. When dry, they are removed from the molds. To build the structure, the bricks are layered to form walls three- to four-feet thick at ground level. The walls are then plastered with a lime and whitewash mixture and the structure is roofed with clay tiles. The hardest part may be extracting the juice from thorny cacti!

Date Nut Bread

1 cup chopped dates
3/4 cup chopped walnuts
3 tablespoons butter
1 1/2 teaspoons baking soda
3/4 cup boiling water

2 eggs
1 teaspoon vanilla extract
1 1/2 cups all-purpose flour
1 cup sugar

Mix the dates, walnuts, butter and baking soda in a large bowl. Add the boiling water and stir until the butter melts and the baking soda dissolves. Let stand for 30 minutes. Preheat the oven to 350 degrees. Beat the eggs and vanilla in a bowl with a fork. Add to the date mixture and mix well. Stir in the flour and sugar. Spoon into a large loaf pan sprayed with nonstick baking spray with flour. Bake for 1 hour. Cool in the pan for several minutes and remove to a wire rack to cool completely.

Serves 8 to 10

Zucchini Bread

3 cups all-purpose flour
1 teaspoon baking soda
1 teaspoon ground cinnamon
1 teaspoon grated nutmeg
1/4 teaspoon salt
3 eggs

1 2/3 cups sugar
3/4 cup vegetable oil
2 cups grated zucchini
3/4 cup chopped walnuts
3/4 cup raisins

Preheat the oven to 350 degrees. Sift the flour, baking soda, cinnamon, nutmeg and salt together. Beat the eggs in a mixing bowl until foamy. Add the sugar and oil and mix well. Add the flour mixture and mix until blended. Stir in the zucchini, walnuts and raisins. Pour into two large foil loaf pans sprayed with nonstick cooking spray. Bake for 1 hour or until the loaves test done.

Makes 2 loaves

Oatmeal Blueberry Muffins

1 1/3 cups all-purpose flour

3/4 cup quick-cooking oats

2 teaspoons baking powder

1/2 teaspoon baking soda

1/4 teaspoon salt

1 egg, beaten

3/4 cup milk

1/2 cup packed brown sugar

1/4 cup vegetable oil

1/2 teaspoon vanilla extract

3/4 cup fresh or thawed frozen blueberries

Preheat the oven to 400 degrees. Mix the flour, oats, baking powder, baking soda and salt in a large bowl. Add the egg, milk, brown sugar, oil and vanilla and mix well. Fold in the blueberries. Spoon into greased and floured muffin cups. Bake for 16 to 18 minutes or until golden brown.

Makes 12 muffins

The Bells are Ringing
A CALL TO TABLE

The Founding Document

Mission San Juan Capistrano was officially founded on November 1, 1776, by Padre President Juniperro Serra and named by the Spanish Viceroy Bucareli. Part of the original Founding Document, penned by Fr. Serra, reads like the ingredients in a recipe.

continued ➤

Poppy Seed Orange Muffins

1¹/3 cups all-purpose flour

1 cup sugar

¹/2 teaspoon baking soda

1 tablespoon poppy seeds

¹/2 teaspoon salt

2 tablespoons grated orange zest

¹/2 cup sour cream

¹/3 cup butter, softened

2 tablespoons orange juice

1 egg

6 orange sections, finely chopped

Preheat the oven to 400 degrees. Mix the flour, sugar, baking soda, poppy seeds, salt and orange zest in a mixing bowl. Add the sour cream, butter, orange juice and egg and mix at low speed until moistened. Stir in the oranges. Spoon into foil-lined muffin cups. Bake for 20 minutes.

Note: You may use 2 tablespoons reserved juice and 6 orange sections from a can of mandarin oranges if preferred.

Makes 12 muffins

Streusel Coffee Cake Muffins

Streusel Topping

3 tablespoons unsalted butter,
   softened

1/4 cup packed brown sugar

1/4 cup quick-cooking oats

1/4 cup all-purpose flour

1/4 cup finely chopped walnuts

1/2 teaspoon ground cinnamon

1/4 teaspoon grated nutmeg

Muffins

2 cups all-purpose flour

1 tablespoon baking powder

1/2 teaspoon baking soda

1 teaspoon ground cinnamon

1/2 teaspoon grated nutmeg

1/4 teaspoon salt

2/3 cup packed brown sugar

1 cup buttermilk

1 egg

1 teaspoon vanilla extract

1/2 cup (1 stick) unsalted butter,
   melted and cooled

For the topping, mix the butter, brown sugar, oats, flour, walnuts, cinnamon and nutmeg in a bowl and set aside.

For the muffins, preheat the oven to 375 degrees. Sift the flour, baking powder, baking soda, cinnamon, nutmeg and salt into a bowl. Mix in the brown sugar. Blend the buttermilk, egg and vanilla in a small bowl. Add to the dry ingredients and mix well. Stir in the butter.

Spoon the batter into paper-lined muffin cups. Sprinkle with the topping. Bake for 25 to 35 minutes or until golden brown and a wooden pick inserted into the center of a muffin comes out clean.

Makes 12 muffins

Founding Items for the Mission

2 families of husband and wife
   (lay helpers to the padres)

4 Indian boys, unmarried

4 measures of fine flour

2 measures of unsifted flour

3 measures of beans and 1 of rice

4 strings of colored beads to trade
   with the native people

9 milk cows

1 yoke of oxen

8 pack mules

3 saddle mules

3 horses and 2 mares, 1 with colt

1 male and 1 female pig

chickens

saddles and trappings and bridles

12 new large hoes

2 axes

6 machetes

6 knives

1 branding iron with the mark "CA"

The Bells are Ringing
A CALL TO TABLE

La Pozolera

Not far from the "patio" was the outdoor community kitchen, La Pozolera. During the Mission's most prosperous time, this kitchen fed up to one thousand people three times a day. Women roasted corn, shelled beans and peas, and chopped vegetables. They cooked stews using the Mission's livestock and wild game. Cheese was made there and bread was baked in the hornos. Olive oil, from the Mission's own press, was vital for cooking. One can just imagine the tempting aromas emanating constantly from La Pozolera! Whole Kernel Corn Muffins are guaranteed to provide delicious aromas of their own and turn your kitchen into a Mission Pozolera.

24

Whole Kernel Corn Muffins

1 cup all-purpose flour
3/4 cup cornmeal
3 tablespoons sugar
2 teaspoons baking powder
1/4 teaspoon salt
1 egg, beaten

3/4 cup milk
1/4 cup vegetable oil
1 (8-ounce) can whole kernel corn, drained
2 tablespoons finely chopped chives or green onions

Preheat the oven to 400 degrees. Mix the flour, cornmeal, sugar, baking powder and salt in a large bowl. Combine the egg, milk and oil in a bowl and mix well. Add to the dry ingredients and mix well. Fold in the corn and chives.

Spoon the batter into greased muffin cups, filling two-thirds full. Bake for 18 to 20 minutes or until a wooden pick inserted into the center of a muffin comes out clean. Serve with a bowl of hot chili.

Serves 8 to 10

Ron Bauer, Living History Volunteer, at the outdoor oven

Scones

2 cups all-purpose flour
2 1/2 teaspoons baking powder
2 tablespoons sugar
1 teaspoon salt
1/4 cup (1/2 stick) butter
1 egg

1/2 cup milk
1/2 cup currants, dried cherries, dried
    cranberries, nuts or chocolate
    chips (optional)
egg white or milk for brushing
sugar for sprinkling

Preheat the oven to 375 degrees. Mix the flour, baking powder, 2 tablespoons sugar and the salt in a mixing bowl or food processor. Add the butter and cut in with knives or process until crumbly. Add the egg and 1/2 cup milk and mix well. Fold in the currants. Drop by tablespoonfuls onto baking parchment-lined baking sheets. Brush the tops with egg white or additional milk and sprinkle with additional sugar. Bake for 20 minutes.

Serves 8 to 10

Oatmeal Yeast Bread

1 envelope dry yeast
1/3 cup lukewarm water
2 cups boiling water
1 cup quick-cooking oats
1/4 cup packed brown sugar

1/2 cup shortening, or 1/2 cup (1 stick) butter
2 1/4 teaspoons salt
5 to 6 cups all-purpose flour
melted butter

Dissolve the yeast in the lukewarm water in a bowl. Pour the boiling water over the oats in a large bowl. Add the brown sugar, shortening and salt and mix well. Let stand until cool. Stir in the yeast mixture. Add enough of the flour to form a soft dough and beat thoroughly for 10 minutes. Add enough of the remaining flour to form a stiff dough and knead until smooth. Place in a greased bowl, turning to coat the surface. Cover and let rise in a warm place until doubled in bulk. Knead the dough once and let rise until doubled in bulk. Divide the dough into two equal portions. Shape each portion into a loaf and place in two 4×9-inch foil loaf pans sprayed with nonstick cooking spray. Let rise until doubled in bulk. Preheat the oven to 350 degrees. Bake for 35 to 40 minutes or until golden brown. Remove from the oven and brush with melted butter.

The Bells are Ringing
A CALL TO TABLE

Makes 2 loaves

Fig and Pecan Jam

5 cups ripe black Mission figs

1 cup chopped pecans

1/2 cup fresh lemon juice

1/2 cup water

1 box pectin

3 3/4 cups sugar

Trim the stem ends from the figs and finely chop or grind the fruit. Combine with the pecans, lemon juice and water in a 6- to 8-quart saucepan. Stir in the pectin and 1/4 cup of the sugar. Bring to a boil. Stir in the remaining 3 1/2 cups sugar and return to a hard boil. Boil for 1 minute, stirring constantly; the mixture will be thick.

Ladle the mixture into hot sterilized jars, leaving 1/2 inch headspace; wipe the edges. Seal with sterilized lids. Let stand until cool and check the lids for a tight seal. Serve with meats or as filling for cookies and cakes.

Note: You can use dried figs when fresh figs are not available, preparing as above.

Makes 8 large jars or 12 small jars

Plum and Pear Jam

5 pounds mixture of plums and pears
1 cup water

1 box pectin
6^1/$_2$ cups sugar

Cut the unpeeled plums and pears into quarters, discarding the seeds and pits. Combine with the water in a large saucepan. Bring to a simmer and simmer until tender. Remove to a blender and process until smooth.

Measure 5^1/$_2$ cups of the fruit and juice and pour into a saucepan. Add the pectin and bring to a full rolling boil. Stir in the sugar and return to a full boil. Boil for 1 minute. Ladle into sterilized jars, leaving ^{1}/$_2$ inch headspace; wipe the jars. Seal with sterilized lids.

Makes 6 to 8 jars

Orange Lemon Marmalade

4 oranges
2 lemons
^{1}/$_8$ teaspoon baking soda

2^1/$_2$ cups water
1 box pectin
5^1/$_2$ cups sugar

Remove the zest from the oranges and lemons using a vegetable peeler and chop. Peel and discard the remaining white part of the peel from the fruit. Chop the fruit pulp in a bowl, reserving any juices. Place the orange zest, lemon zest and baking soda in a saucepan and add the water. Bring to a boil and reduce the heat. Cover and simmer for 20 minutes. Add the undrained chopped fruit and simmer for 10 minutes. Remove from the heat. Measure 4 cups cooked fruit and pour into a saucepan. Stir in the pectin. Bring to a full rolling boil, stirring constantly. Remove from the heat. Ladle into hot sterilized jars, leaving ^{1}/$_2$ inch headspace; wipe the edges. Seal with sterilized lids. Let stand for 4 to 5 hours. Store in a cool, dark place. It sometimes takes 2 weeks to set.

Makes 4 to 5 jars

Hides and Tallow

*Cattle meant wealth to the Mission.
The meat ensured that the Mission
workforce remained healthy and
productive. The hides and
tallow were assets to be traded for
such items as tools, utensils, fabrics,
spices, books, and ink.
The hides were tanned at the Mission.
Fat from butchered livestock was
melted into tallow for candles, soap,
axle grease, ointments, and many
other useful items.
When Spanish trading ships came
into port, leather and tallow were
carried to the sea by oxen, and the
bartering for the items needed
at the Mission began.*

Alsatian Cheese Tart

*1 cup sliced onion
1 cup sliced mushrooms
1/4 cup (1/2 stick) butter
1 unbaked (9-inch) pie shell
1 cup (4 ounces) shredded Swiss cheese
1 tablespoon all-purpose flour
4 eggs
13/4 cups cream or heavy cream
1 teaspoon salt
1/4 teaspoon grated nutmeg
1/8 teaspoon pepper
several drops of Tabasco sauce*

Preheat the oven to 350 degrees. Sauté the onion and mushrooms in the butter in a skillet for 5 minutes. Spoon into the pie shell. Toss the cheese with the flour and sprinkle over the onion and mushrooms.

Beat the eggs in a bowl. Add the cream, salt, nutmeg, pepper and Tabasco sauce and mix well. Pour into the pie shell. Bake for 40 to 45 minutes or until the filling is firm in the center and the pie shell is golden brown. Serve with a green salad and rolls.

Serves 6 to 8

Baked Eggs with Leeks and Tarragon

4 tablespoons (1/2 stick) butter, softened

3 large leeks, chopped

1 1/2 cups (6 ounces) grated Gruyère cheese

1/2 cup (2 ounces) grated Parmesan cheese or Romano cheese

8 eggs

2 cups cream or heavy cream

2 tablespoons plus 2 teaspoons chopped fresh tarragon

1/2 teaspoon salt

1/4 teaspoon white pepper

Preheat the oven to 375 degrees. Spread 1 tablespoon of the butter in a 9×13-inch baking dish. Melt the remaining 3 tablespoons butter in a large skillet over medium-high heat. Add the leeks and sauté for 5 minutes or until tender. Spread in the prepared baking dish.

Mix the Gruyère and Parmesan cheeses in a bowl. Reserve 1/2 cup of the cheese mixture for the topping and sprinkle the remaining cheese over the leeks. Whisk the eggs, cream, tarragon, salt and white pepper together in a large bowl. Pour over the cheese.

Bake for 30 minutes or until the center is set and the top is golden brown. Sprinkle with the reserved cheese mixture and bake for 5 minutes longer or until the cheeses melt.

Serves 8

Ham and Cheese Casserole

3 cups cubed day-old crusty French bread

3 cups chopped cooked ham

2 cups (8 ounces) shredded sharp
   Cheddar cheese

2 tablespoons all-purpose flour

2 tablespoons butter, melted

3 cups milk

1 tablespoon dry mustard

1 teaspoon Tabasco sauce

Layer the bread cubes, ham and cheese in a 9×13-inch baking dish. Mix the flour, butter, milk, dry mustard and Tabasco sauce in a blender and process for 1 minute. Pour over the layers in the baking dish. Chill in the refrigerator for 8 hours or longer. Preheat the oven to 350 degrees. Bake the casserole for 1 hour.

Note: This make-ahead brunch casserole contains no eggs.

Serves 6 to 8

California Egg Puff

10 eggs
1/2 cup all-purpose flour
1 teaspoon baking powder
4 cups (16 ounces) shredded
   Monterey Jack cheese

1/2 cup (1 stick) butter, melted
1 (4-ounce) can chopped green chiles
1/2 teaspoon salt
2 cups creamed cottage cheese

Preheat the oven to 350 degrees. Beat the eggs in a bowl until light and frothy. Add the flour, baking powder, Monterey Jack cheese, butter, green chiles and salt; mix well. Fold in the cottage cheese.

Spoon the cheese mixture into a greased 9×12-inch baking dish. Bake for 25 to 30 minutes or until puffed and light brown. Cut into squares and serve hot.

Note: You can also serve creamed chicken with the dish to transform it into a lunch entrée.

Serves 8 to 10

Cheese Strata

8 slices white sandwich bread
2 cups (8 ounces) shredded sharp
   Cheddar cheese
1 cup milk
1 cup half-and-half

4 eggs
Tabasco sauce to taste
salt and pepper to taste
1/4 cup chopped chives

Cut the bread into large cubes. Layer the bread cubes and cheese one-half at a time in a buttered 10-inch baking dish with a 3-inch depth. Beat the milk, half-and-half, eggs, Tabasco sauce, salt and pepper in a bowl. Pour over the layers. Cover and chill for 8 to 10 hours. Preheat the oven to 325 degrees. Sprinkle the chives over the strata. Bake for 1 hour or until golden brown and puffy.

Serves 6 to 8

The Bells are Ringing
A CALL TO TABLE

Mexican Crepes

Cheese Sauce

1/2 cup (1 stick) butter

1/2 cup all-purpose flour

1 quart (4 cups) milk

2 cups (8 ounces) shredded Cheddar cheese

1 teaspoon dry mustard

1/2 teaspoon salt

pepper to taste

Crepes

12 thin slices ham

12 flour tortillas

1 pound Monterey Jack cheese, cut into

*   1 1/2×4-inch sticks*

1 (4-ounce) can whole green chiles,

*   cut into 3/4-inch-wide strips*

paprika to taste

For the cheese sauce, melt the butter in a 2-quart saucepan. Stir in the flour and cook for 2 minutes, stirring constantly. Add the milk and cook until thickened, stirring constantly. Cook and stir for 1 to 2 minutes longer. Remove from the heat and stir in the cheese, dry mustard, salt and pepper.

For the crepes, preheat the oven to 350 degrees. Place one slice of ham on each tortilla. Top with a cheese stick and a green chile strip. Roll up the tortillas to enclose the filling and arrange seam side down in a 9×13-inch baking dish. Spoon the cheese sauce over the crepes and sprinkle with paprika. Bake for 45 minutes.

Note: You can prepare this dish a day ahead, refrigerating the tortilla rolls and cheese sauce separately. Top the rolls with the cheese sauce just before baking and adjust the baking time for the chilled ingredients.

Makes 12

Crème Brûlée French Toast

1 cup (2 sticks) unsalted butter

2 cups packed brown sugar

1/4 cup corn syrup

2 large loaves egg bread

6 eggs

1 1/2 cups half-and-half

1 1/2 cups heavy cream

2 teaspoons orange juice

1 teaspoon vanilla extract

2 tablespoons chopped hazelnuts

1/2 teaspoon salt

Combine the butter, brown sugar and corn syrup in a small heavy saucepan. Cook over medium heat until the butter melts and the brown sugar dissolves, whisking constantly. Pour one-third of the mixture into a 9×13-inch baking dish.

Cut each bread loaf into six 1-inch slices, discarding the ends or reserving them for another use. Arrange six slices in a single layer in the prepared baking dish. Drizzle with half the remaining brown sugar mixture.

Whisk the eggs, half-and-half, cream, orange juice, vanilla, hazelnuts and salt together in a bowl. Pour half the mixture over the bread layer in the baking pan. Layer the remaining bread slices in the pan and top with the remaining brown sugar mixture and then the remaining egg mixture. Chill, covered, for 8 hours or longer.

Preheat the oven to 350 degrees. Let the layers stand until room temperature. Add a small amount of additional cream or half-and-half if the mixture appears dry. Bake on the center oven rack for 40 to 45 minutes or until the center is puffed and the edges are pale golden brown.

Note: You can also top with pecans or serve with toasted pecans and fresh berries.

Serves 8 to 10

Magdalena: Legendary Mission Ghost

According to legend, young Magdalena and Teofilo were lovers. When their affair was discovered, she was required to repent of her sins before the congregation. On December 8, 1812, she is reported to have begun her "walk of shame," when suddenly the earth rumbled, and the walls came crashing down. Magdalena was found in the rubble and by her side was the body of Teofilo, who had tried to save her. Today, old-time residents claim that Magdalena can be seen some moonlit nights in the one remaining window in the Old Stone Church, face aglow, waiting for Teofilo.

"Those" Potatoes

Crunch Topping
  2 cups crushed cornflakes
  1/4 cup (1/2 stick) butter, melted

Potatoes
  1 (2-pound) package frozen hash brown or O'Brien potatoes, thawed
  2 cups sour cream

  1 (10-ounce) can cream of mushroom or cream of chicken soup
  1/2 cup (1 stick) butter, melted
  1/2 cup chopped onion
  2 cups (8 ounces) shredded Cheddar cheese
  seasoned salt and pepper to taste

For the topping, mix the cornflakes and butter in a bowl and set aside.

For the potatoes, preheat the oven to 350 degrees. Combine the potatoes with the sour cream, soup and butter in a large bowl and mix well. Stir in the onion, cheese, seasoned salt and pepper.

Spread the potato mixture in a greased 9×13-inch baking dish. Sprinkle with the topping. Bake for 45 to 55 minutes or until bubbly and golden brown.

Serves 8

Bell Wall and remains of the "Old Stone Church"

Potato Quiche

Potato Crust

1 (16-ounce) package frozen shredded hash brown potatoes, thawed

1/2 cup (1 stick) butter, melted

11/2 teaspoons beef bouillon granules

Quiche Filling

4 eggs, beaten

1/3 cup finely chopped onion

2 cups creamed cottage cheese

1 cup (4 ounces) shredded Monterey Jack cheese

For the crust, preheat the oven to 400 degrees. Combine the potatoes, butter and bouillon granules in a bowl and mix well. Press the mixture over the bottom and side of a greased 10-inch pie plate to form a crust. Bake for 20 to 25 minutes or until light brown. Remove from the oven.

For the quiche, reduce the oven temperature to 350 degrees. Combine the eggs, onion, cottage cheese and Monterey Jack cheese in a bowl and mix well. Spoon into the potato crust. Bake for 30 to 35 minutes or until puffed and golden brown.

Serves 8 to 10

Tostada Quiche

Guacamole

2 avocados, mashed

1 garlic clove, minced

3 tablespoons lemon juice

1 tomato, peeled, seeded and chopped

1/2 (4-ounce) can chopped green chiles

1/4 teaspoon hot red pepper sauce

salt and pepper to taste

Quiche

1 frozen (9-inch) deep-dish pie shell

8 ounces ground beef or chopped chorizo

1/4 cup chopped onion

1/2 (4-ounce) can chopped green chiles

2 tablespoons taco seasoning mix

1 1/2 cups (6 ounces) shredded
   Cheddar cheese

3 eggs

1 1/2 cups half-and-half

1/2 teaspoon salt

1/8 teaspoon pepper

shredded lettuce and chopped tomato

For the guacamole, combine the avocados, garlic, lemon juice, tomato, green chiles and hot sauce in a bowl. Season with salt and pepper and mix well. Cover and chill until needed.

For the quiche, preheat the oven to 400 degrees. Let the pie shell stand at room temperature for 10 minutes. Bake the pie shell for 7 minutes; remove from the oven.

Reduce the oven temperature to 375 degrees. Combine the ground beef, onion, green chiles and taco seasoning mix in a skillet and cook over medium heat until the ground beef is brown and the onion is tender; drain. Layer the ground beef mixture and the cheese one-third at a time in the prepared pie shell.

Beat the eggs with the half-and-half, salt and pepper in a bowl. Pour over the layers in the pie shell. Bake for 45 minutes or until set. Let stand for 10 minutes before slicing. Top with the guacamole, shredded lettuce and chopped tomato.

Serves 6

Granola

2 cups quick-cooking oats
3/4 cup nuts
3/4 cup shredded coconut
1/2 cup wheat germ
1/2 cup All-Bran cereal
1/2 cup dried cranberries

1/4 cup sesame seeds
1/4 cup honey
2 tablespoons brown sugar
1/4 cup canola oil or safflower oil
1/2 teaspoon vanilla extract

Preheat the oven to 325 degrees. Combine the oats, nuts, coconut, wheat germ, cereal, cranberries and sesame seeds in a bowl and mix well. Combine the honey, brown sugar, canola oil and vanilla in a saucepan and mix well. Cook until heated through. Pour over the dry ingredients and stir gently to mix.

Spread the mixture on a baking sheet. Bake for 20 minutes or until crisp, stirring every 8 minutes. Remove from the oven and break apart. Let stand until cool and store in an airtight container.

Makes 5 cups

Living History Volunteers, stomping grapes for the 2003 "Vintage Event" at the Mission

Mission Winery

Many historians believe that the California wine industry began at Mission San Juan Capistrano. Cuttings from Mexico were planted at the Mission around 1779. Written records indicate that a winery that produced sacramental wine and brandy was built at the Mission in 1783. In recent years, members of the Mission's Living History Society have tried their hands at re-creating the wine making process at the Mission, complete with old-fashioned grape stomping.

The Bells are Ringing
A CALL TO TABLE

Pirates and Treasure

Early one morning in December of 1818, two pirate ships anchored in San Juan Capistrano Bay, now Dana Point. The leader of this band of pirates, a former French captain turned privateer, Hippolyte Bouchard, demanded that the town surrender its valuables or risk being plundered and burned. When the pirates arrived in the town, they found it empty.

continued ➤

Marmalade Fruit Bake

1 (11-ounce) can
   mandarin oranges
2 (16-ounce) cans pear
   halves, drained
2 (16-ounce) cans peach
   halves, drained

$^2/_3$ cup orange marmalade or
   lemon marmalade
2 teaspoons cornstarch
$1^1/_2$ teaspoons minced fresh
   mint leaves

Preheat the oven to 325 degrees. Drain the mandarin oranges, reserving $1/2$ cup juice and the oranges. Combine the oranges with the pears and peaches in a buttered 9×13-inch baking dish.

Combine the marmalade, reserved orange juice, cornstarch and mint leaves in a small saucepan and mix well. Bring to a boil and cook until thickened, stirring constantly. Pour over the fruit in the baking dish. Bake for 20 minutes. Serve warm with meats and fish.

Note: You can substitute fresh fruits for the canned fruit and white wine or brandy for the orange juice, if preferred.

Serves 8

California Spiced Fruit Salad

$1/3$ cup honey

2 cups water

4 large star anise

1 cinnamon stick

1 vanilla bean

zest from 2 large oranges

5 pounds fruit, such as blueberries, chopped cantaloupe,
    chopped watermelon or chopped honeydew melon

Combine the honey, water, star anise and cinnamon stick in a medium saucepan. Scrape the seeds from the vanilla bean into the mixture and add the bean pod. Bring to a boil, stirring to mix well. Reduce the heat and simmer for 8 minutes or until the liquid is reduced to $1^{1}/2$ cups.

Remove from the heat and add the orange zest. Let stand until cool. Strain, discarding the solids. Combine the liquid with the fruit in a bowl. Marinate in the refrigerator for 4 hours or longer.

Serves 8 to 10

The townsfolk had been warned well ahead of time, had removed all valuables to safety, and had gone into hiding. The angry band plundered what they could from the homes and then raided the stores of food and wine at the Mission. Three days later, now sated and sober, they replenished their ship's supplies from the Mission stores and sailed away. Townspeople and the Mission Padres retrieved their valuables and set about repairing the town. Today rumors persist that some of the hidden valuables were never found.

The Bells are Ringing
A CALL TO TABLE

A Call to Lunch

Refresh & Refuel

The ruins of the Great Stone Church are considered one of the top one hundred most endangered places in the world according to the World Monument Fund. Construction began on the Stone Church in 1797. Master stonemason from Mexico Isidro Aguilar traveled to San Juan Capistrano to oversee construction. The Mission Indians, "the Juanenos" (the term used for Acjachemen after the founding of the Mission), provided the labor, quarrying stone from miles away and using carts, donkeys, and oxen to carry the stone to the Mission. The Church was dedicated in 1806 as the largest building and the only stone church in California. Six years later, on December 8, 1812, an earthquake struck, collapsing the south and west walls and killing forty-two people who had gathered for a Feast Day Mass.

The bells call us back to table now with lighter, luncheon-type fare. Here you will find some delicious recipes, as well as more historical tidbits from the second mission period, The Rancho Period. The Rancho Period includes the time from Mexican Independence from Spain in 1821, until President Lincoln's return of the control of the Mission to the Catholic Church, in 1865.

Crab Meat or Lobster Bisque

1/2 cup finely chopped celery

1/4 cup chopped sweet onion

1/4 cup (1/2 stick) butter

2 tablespoons all-purpose flour

4 cups half-and-half

1 pound crab meat or lobster meat

1 teaspoon salt

1/4 cup pale dry sherry

paprika to taste

Sauté the celery and onion in the butter in a saucepan until tender. Stir in the flour. Cook for several minutes, stirring constantly. Add the half-and-half gradually, cooking until the mixture thickens and stirring constantly.

Stir in the crab meat and salt. Heat over low heat until serving time, taking care not to burn it. Stir in the sherry. Ladle into serving bowls and sprinkle with paprika to serve.

Serves 4 to 6

Quick Clam Chowder

1 carrot, shredded

1 rib celery, finely chopped

2 tablespoons chopped onion

2 tablespoons butter

2 slices bacon, chopped and cooked (optional)

1 (6-ounce) can minced clams

1 1/4 cups (or more) half-and-half

red pepper to taste

Sauté the carrot, celery and onion in the butter in a saucepan until tender. Add the bacon, undrained clams, half-and-half and red pepper. Bring just to a boil, stirring to mix well. Ladle into serving bowls and serve with salad and bread.

Serves 2 to 4

The Bells are Ringing
A CALL TO TABLE

Corn Chowder

1/2 cup chopped yellow onion
1/2 cup chopped celery
1/4 cup chopped bacon
1 cup finely chopped potato
1 cup water

2 (10-ounce) cans cream of
    corn soup
1/2 teaspoon salt
pepper to taste
2 cups half-and-half

Sauté the onion and celery with the bacon in a 2-quart saucepan until the bacon is crisp and the vegetables are tender. Add the potato, water, soup, salt and pepper; mix well. Simmer until the potatoes are tender. Stir in the half-and-half and simmer just until heated through. Ladle into soup bowls to serve.

Serves 6

Asparagus Soup

1/2 cup chopped onion
2 tablespoons butter
3 pounds fresh asparagus
2 cups water

1/2 teaspoon salt
2 1/2 cups half-and-half
salt and pepper to taste

Sauté the onion in the butter in a small skillet until translucent. Rinse the asparagus and snap off the tough ends. Remove the scales from the stalks with a vegetable peeler, if desired. Cut the asparagus into 1-inch pieces. Place the asparagus, water and 1/2 teaspoon salt in a large saucepan and cook over medium heat until tender; drain. Heat 1 cup of the half-and half. Process the drained asparagus, sautéed onion and the hot half-and-half in a blender until smooth. Return to the saucepan and add the remaining 1 1/2 cups half-and-half. Cook until heated through. Season with salt and pepper.

Makes 2 quarts

Fate of Mission San Juan Capistrano

When Mission San Juan Capistrano was stripped of its grazing lands, it began to fall into ruin. In 1845 an Englishman, John Forster, who had married the sister of Pio Pico, the Mexican governor of California, purchased the run-down mission for $710. Don Juan Forster lived there with his wife Ysidora and their sons until 1864. Don Juan's great-great grandson, Tony Forster, still lives in San Juan Capistrano along with other descendants of the Forster family.

Beefy Cabbage Soup

1 cabbage

1¹/2 pounds lean ground beef

1 (28-ounce) can diced tomatoes

1 envelope Italian salad dressing mix

1 (10-ounce) can tomatoes with green chiles

2 (15-ounce) cans red kidney beans, drained

1 (46-ounce) can vegetable juice cocktail

Cut the cabbage into quarters and coarsely chop. Brown the ground beef in a stockpot, stirring with a wooden spoon until crumbly. Add the cabbage, tomatoes, salad dressing mix, tomatoes with green chiles, beans and vegetable juice cocktail. Simmer for 1 hour. Ladle into soup bowls and serve with warm crusty bread.

Serves 6 to 8

Cream of Broccoli Soup

2 tablespoons minced onion

¹/4 cup (¹/2 stick) butter

¹/3 cup all-purpose flour

4 cups milk

2 tablespoons dry mustard

¹/4 teaspoon salt

¹/8 teaspoon pepper

2 to 3 cups drained cooked broccoli

1 cup (4 ounces) cubed Velveeta cheese

Sauté the onion in the butter in a large saucepan. Stir in the flour and cook until bubbly. Stir in the milk, dry mustard, salt and pepper gradually, stirring constantly. Bring to a boil and cook until thickened, stirring constantly. Add the broccoli. Pour into a food processor and process until smooth. Return to the saucepan and add the cheese. Cook over low heat until the cheese melts and the soup is heated through, stirring to mix well. Ladle into soup bowls.

Note: You can substitute cauliflower or asparagus for the broccoli in this recipe. It can be prepared in advance and reheated to serve.

Serves 4 to 6

The Bells are Ringing
A CALL TO TABLE

Cauliflower and Leek Soup

1 leek, white and pale green parts only

1 teaspoon unsalted butter

1 tablespoon water

1 head cauliflower, cored and cut into 1-inch chunks (6 cups)

1/2 teaspoon dried dill weed

2 cups homemade or canned chicken broth

1 1/4 cups whole milk or low-fat milk

1 1/4 teaspoons salt

freshly ground pepper to taste

1 to 2 tablespoons sliced almonds, toasted

Cut the leek into halves lengthwise and rinse under running water. Cut the halves crosswise into slices 1/2 inch thick and pat dry. Melt the butter in the water in a 4-quart heavy saucepan or stockpot over medium heat. Add the cauliflower and leek. Cook for 5 minutes or until the cauliflower begins to soften, stirring occasionally. Do not brown. Add the dill weed and cook for 1 minute, stirring constantly. Add the broth, milk, salt and pepper and bring to a simmer, stirring occasionally. Reduce the heat and gently simmer, covered, for 20 minutes or until the cauliflower is very tender, stirring occasionally. Purée the soup in two or three batches in a blender. Reheat the soup and adjust the seasonings if needed. Ladle into soup bowls and sprinkle with the almonds.

Serves 4

Gazpacho

1 garlic clove
1/2 teaspoon salt
1 1/2 cucumbers, peeled, seeded and chopped
1 1/2 large tomatoes, peeled and chopped
1 mild onion, finely chopped
3/4 cup finely chopped celery
1 red bell pepper, finely chopped
1/2 green bell pepper, finely chopped
1 (4-ounce) can chopped green chiles, drained
2 jalapeño chiles, seeded and minced

2 tablespoons chopped fresh cilantro, or to taste
2 (14-ounce) cans fat-free chicken broth, or
   3 3/4 cup defatted homemade chicken broth
1 (48-ounce) can tomato juice
3 tablespoons fresh lemon juice
1 tablespoon fresh lime juice
1/4 cup virgin olive oil
1 1/2 teaspoons sugar
2 teaspoons cumin
seasoned salt to taste

Mash the garlic with the salt. Combine the garlic, cucumbers, tomatoes, onion, celery, red bell pepper, green bell pepper, green chiles, jalapeño chiles and cilantro in a large bowl. Add the broth, tomato juice, lemon juice, lime juice, olive oil, sugar, cumin and seasoned salt; mix well. Chill for several hours to develop the flavors.

Serve plain or add toppings such as sour cream, crushed tortilla chips, shredded Cheddar cheese, garlic croutons, chopped avocado and/or chopped cooked bacon.

Note: This is a good dish to take in a thermos to football games, picnics, Music Under the Stars concerts, or the Hollywood Bowl.

Serves 8 to 10

The Bells are Ringing
A CALL TO TABLE

Italian Sausage and Lentil Soup

8 ounces sweet Italian sausage, casings removed

2 carrots, sliced (about 1 cup)

1 rib celery, sliced (about 1/2 cup)

1 small onion, chopped (about 1/3 cup)

1 tablespoon olive oil

5 cups water

1/2 small head cabbage, chopped (about 4 cups)

1 cup dried lentils, rinsed and drained

1 cup tomato purée

1 1/2 teaspoons sugar

1 1/2 teaspoons salt

1/2 teaspoon crushed oregano

1/4 teaspoon pepper

Sauté the sausage in a large saucepan until brown and crumbly; drain. Add the carrots, celery, onion and olive oil and sauté for 5 minutes or until the vegetables are tender-crisp. Add the water, cabbage, lentils, tomato purée, sugar, salt, oregano and pepper. Mix well and bring to a boil. Reduce the heat and simmer, covered, for 45 minutes or until the lentils are tender. Ladle into soup bowls.

Serves 5

Baked Onion Soup

4 large Vidalia onions, sliced 1/2 inch thick
1/2 cup (1 stick) butter
2 tablespoons all-purpose flour
2/3 cup chicken broth or vegetable bouillon
1 tablespoon sherry, or to taste
1 1/2 cups soft bread crumbs
1/2 cup (2 ounces) shredded sharp Cheddar cheese
2 tablespoons grated Parmesan cheese

Preheat the oven to 350 degrees. Sauté the onions in the butter in a large saucepan until translucent but not brown. Add the flour and cook until light golden brown, stirring constantly to prevent burning. Stir in the broth and sherry. Cook until slightly thickened, stirring constantly.

Spoon the soup into a greased baking dish and top with the bread crumbs, Cheddar cheese and Parmesan cheese. Bake for 30 minutes or until the top is golden brown.

Note: This can be prepared in advance and chilled until baking time.

Serves 6 to 8

Mushroom Soup

1 onion, minced

2 to 3 cups sliced mushrooms

1/4 cup (1/2 stick) butter

1/3 cup all-purpose flour

4 cups half-and-half

1/4 teaspoon salt

1/8 teaspoon pepper

1 red bell pepper, chopped

1/2 cup chopped parsley

Sauté the onion and mushrooms in the butter in a large saucepan until tender. Stir in the flour and cook until bubbly. Stir in the half-and-half, salt and pepper gradually. Bring to a boil and cook until thickened, stirring constantly. Ladle into serving bowls and top with the bell pepper and parsley.

Note: This can be prepared in advance and reheated to serve.

Serves 4 to 6

Swedish Pea Soup

2 cups dried yellow peas
1 carrot, finely chopped
1 small yellow onion, finely chopped
1 ham bone
1/4 teaspoon ground ginger
6 cups cold water
1 cup cream or heavy cream
salt and pepper to taste
grated nutmeg to taste

Soak the peas in water to cover in a bowl for 8 hours or longer; drain. Combine the peas with the carrot, onion, ham bone, ginger and cold water in a saucepan. Simmer until the peas are very tender. Remove and discard the ham bone.

Pour the soup into a blender and process until smooth. Return to the saucepan and stir in the cream; season with salt and pepper. Simmer just until heated through. Ladle into small soup bowls and sprinkle with nutmeg.

Note: Serve this as the first course in small espresso cups either before coming to the table or at the table for a very special party.

Serves 8

Potato and Leek Soup

4 large potatoes, peeled and cut into quarters

1 cup chopped leeks, white parts only

2 tablespoons butter

1³/4 cups chicken broth

1³/4 cups water

1 teaspoon salt

1 (12-ounce) can evaporated milk, or 1¹/2 cups cream

2 cups milk

salt and pepper to taste

Cook the potatoes in enough water to cover in a saucepan until very tender; drain. Sauté the leeks in the butter in a saucepan until translucent. Add the broth, water and 1 teaspoon salt; mix well. Pour into a food processor and add the potatoes; process until smooth. Return to the saucepan and stir in the evaporated milk and milk. Heat just to serving temperature and season with additional salt and pepper. Ladle into soup bowls.

Serves 4 to 6

Father Art's Pozole

1 tablespoon vegetable oil
1 (2-pound) pork shoulder, trimmed and
    cut into 1¹/₂-inch cubes
1 large onion, minced
4 garlic cloves, minced
5 cups chicken broth

10 tomatillos, husked, cored and
    cut into quarters
1 bunch cilantro, stems removed
1 (15-ounce) can hominy, drained and rinsed
2 whole dried red chiles, stems removed
salt and pepper to taste

Heat the oil in a large heavy skillet over high heat. Add the pork and sauté until brown on all sides. Reduce the heat to medium and add the onion. Cook for 10 minutes or until the onion is tender, stirring occasionally. Add the garlic and cook for 1 minute. Combine the pork mixture with 3 cups of the chicken broth in a large saucepan. Simmer for 1¹/₂ hours or until the pork is very tender.

Combine the remaining 2 cups chicken broth with the tomatillos and cilantro in a blender and process until puréed. Add the purée, hominy and red chiles to the pork mixture and simmer for 15 minutes. Remove and discard the chiles and season with salt and pepper. Ladle into bowls and serve with chopped onion, shredded lettuce, thinly sliced radishes and lime wedges.

Note: Pozole can be prepared a day or two in advance and chilled, covered, until needed. Reheat over low heat to serve. This is a rustic dish that is ideal for entertaining.

Serves 6

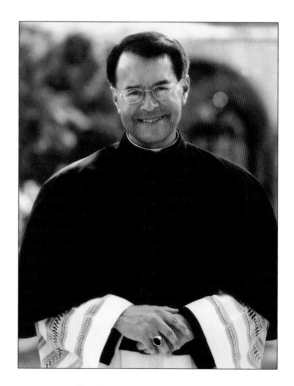

Very Reverend Arthur A. Holquin
Rector/Pastor: Mission Basilica San Juan Caspistrano

Tomato Madrilene

1/4 cup chopped onion

1/4 cup (1/2 stick) butter

2 (18-ounce) cans tomato juice

2 (10-ounce) cans beef broth

1 bay leaf

pinch of sugar

Sauté the onion in the butter in a large saucepan. Add the tomato juice, broth, bay leaf and sugar. Bring just to a boil and reduce the heat. Simmer for 5 minutes; remove and discard the bay leaf. Ladle into soup bowls and garnish with grated Parmesan cheese, chopped parsley and croutons.

Serves 8 to 10

La Canción Malancolica by Theodore Lukits

The Rancho Period

Following Mexico's independence from Spain in 1821, the Mexican government confiscated all mission lands and granted large tracts to private citizens. It was the beginning of the Rancho Period, and the mission way of life gave way to the "rancho" way of life. The one similarity between the two periods was that the rancho was self-sufficient like the mission era before it. Most rancho households consisted of the owner and his family, plus a large number of servants and vaqueros, who were generally Indians who had lived at the missions. The average rancho family could easily exceed one hundred.

Chicken Tortilla Soup

1 cup chopped onion

2 tablespoons olive oil

2 carrots, chopped

2 ribs celery, chopped

2 garlic cloves, minced

6 cups canned or homemade chicken broth

1 (10-ounce) package frozen mixed vegetables

2 or 3 zucchini, chopped

1 (14-ounce) can diced tomatoes

1 (16-ounce) can pinto beans, drained
   and rinsed

1 (12-ounce) jar mild salsa

2 teaspoons cumin

1 teaspoon chili powder, or to taste

1/4 cup chopped cilantro

1 teaspoon salt

1 to 1 1/2 cups cooked white or brown rice

2 cups chopped cooked chicken

salt and pepper to taste

3 tablespoons (or more) vegetable oil

4 corn tortillas, cut into 1/4-inch strips

Sauté the onion in the olive oil in a large saucepan over medium heat until translucent. Add the carrots and celery and sauté for 5 minutes. Reduce the heat and add the garlic. Sauté for 2 minutes longer. Stir in the broth, mixed vegetables, zucchini, tomatoes, beans and salsa.

Bring the soup to a simmer and add the cumin, chili powder, cilantro and 1 teaspoon salt. Simmer for 20 minutes. Stir in the rice and chicken. Season with pepper and additional salt and adjust the other seasonings to taste. Simmer until heated through.

Heat the vegetable oil in a skillet until very hot. Add the tortilla strips in small batches and fry until crisp, adding additional vegetable oil if needed. Drain on paper towels.

Ladle the soup into bowls and top with the tortilla strips. Top with sour cream, shredded Cheddar cheese, chopped green onions, chopped avocado and/or additional chopped cilantro, if desired.

Serves 6 to 8

Basic Pasta Salad

Basic Pasta Dressing

- 1/4 cup red wine vinegar
- 1 tablespoon capers
- 1 garlic clove, minced or pressed
- 1/2 to 3/4 teaspoon kosher salt
- 1/2 teaspoon freshly ground pepper
- 6 tablespoons extra-virgin olive oil

Salad

- 8 ounces fusilli
- salt to taste
- 12 ounces small cherry tomatoes, whole or cut into halves (about 1 1/2 cups)
- 1/4 cup julienned fresh basil
- 1 tablespoon chopped fresh parsley
- 1/2 cup coarsely chopped sweet red onion
- 3 green onions, diagonally sliced
- 1/4 cup (1 ounce) finely grated Parmesan cheese

For the dressing, whisk the vinegar, capers, garlic, kosher salt and pepper together in a bowl. Add the olive oil gradually, whisking constantly.

For the salad, cook the pasta to al dente in salted water in a saucepan, taking care not to overcook; drain. Combine with one-third of the dressing in a bowl and toss to coat well. Add the tomatoes, basil, parsley, red onion, green onions and cheese; toss lightly. Adjust the seasoning and amount of dressing as desired, as the pasta will absorb the dressing as it cools.

Note: Other optional ingredients which can be added include: small cubes of Italian salami, cubes of mozzarella cheese, black salt-cured or Greek kalamata olives, Spanish-style green olives, sliced celery, and/or drained marinated artichoke hearts.

Serves 4

The Bells are Ringing
A CALL TO TABLE

Shrimp Pasta Salad with Almonds and Apricots

Sherry Dressing

    3/4 cup mayonnaise

    3/4 cup sour cream

    3 tablespoons dry sherry

    1 tablespoon lemon juice

    1 teaspoon Dijon mustard

    2 teaspoons grated lemon zest

    1 teaspoon salt

    1/4 teaspoon pepper

Salad

    8 ounces fusilli

    1 pound medium fresh shrimp, cooked, peeled and deveined

    3 cups chopped fresh broccoli

    1 cup chopped celery

    1/2 cup finely chopped green onions

    1 cup dried apricots, cut into strips

    3/4 cup toasted whole almonds

For the dressing, combine the mayonnaise, sour cream, sherry, lemon juice, Dijon mustard, lemon zest, salt and pepper in a bowl; mix well. Store, covered, in the refrigerator until serving time.

For the salad, cook the pasta to al dente using the package directions. Drain in a colander and rinse with cold water. Combine with the shrimp, broccoli, celery, green onions, apricots and almonds; mix lightly. Add the dressing at serving time and toss to coat well.

Serves 6 to 8

Shrimp Louis Summertime Salad

Tangy Dressing

> *1/2 cup mayonnaise*
>
> *1/2 cup sour cream*
>
> *1/4 cup ketchup, or to taste*
>
> *1 tablespoon cream-style horseradish*
>
> *2 tablespoons fresh lemon juice*
>
> *2 teaspoons sugar*
>
> *kosher salt and freshly ground pepper to taste*

Salad

> *4 cups torn butter lettuce*
>
> *4 cups torn hearts of romaine*
>
> *1 cup thinly sliced red cabbage*
>
> *1/2 cup chopped celery*
>
> *1 tablespoon drained capers*
>
> *lettuce leaves*
>
> *1 1/2 pounds shrimp, cooked, peeled and deveined*
>
> *1 avocado, sliced (optional)*
>
> *2 hard-cooked eggs, sliced (optional)*

For the dressing, combine the mayonnaise, sour cream, ketchup, horseradish, lemon juice and sugar in a bowl and whisk to mix well. Season with kosher salt and pepper.

For the salad, combine the butter lettuce and romaine in a bowl and add the cabbage, celery and capers; toss gently. Spoon into a bowl lined with lettuce leaves. Arrange the shrimp, avocado and eggs on top.

Toss the salad lightly with one-fourth of the dressing at serving time and spoon onto salad plates. Serve with the remaining salad dressing and garnish with lemon wedges.

Note: While the avocado and egg are optional ingredients for this salad, they add color and flavor.

Serves 6 to 8

Chinese Chicken Salad

Chinese Dressing

$1/3$ cup seasoned rice vinegar

1 teaspoon soy sauce

1 teaspoon sesame oil

$1^{1}/_{2}$ garlic cloves, minced

1 teaspoon grated fresh ginger

Glazed Chicken

3 tablespoons honey

2 tablespoons soy sauce

$1^{1}/_{2}$ teaspoons sesame oil

4 (4-ounce) skinless chicken breasts

Salad

4 cups torn romaine

4 cups torn iceberg lettuce

1 bunch cilantro, chopped

1 red bell pepper, chopped

$1/4$ cup chopped avocado

1 (11-ounce) can mandarin oranges, drained

$1/3$ cup cashews

1 cup chow mein noodles

For the dressing, combine the vinegar, soy sauce, sesame oil, garlic and ginger in a bowl and whisk until well mixed. Store in the refrigerator.

For the chicken, combine the honey, soy sauce and sesame oil in a bowl and whisk to mix well. Cook the chicken in enough water to cover just until tender; drain. Shred the chicken and drizzle with the honey mixture in a bowl. Chill in the refrigerator for several hours.

For the salad, combine the romaine, iceberg lettuce, cilantro, bell pepper, avocado, oranges, cashews and noodles. Add the chicken and serve with the dressing on the side.

Serves 4

Cedar Creek Inn Curried Chicken Salad

1 bunch parsley

2 (8-ounce) chicken breasts, cooked
   and chopped

1/2 cup chopped celery

1/2 cup chopped green onions

1/2 cup raisins, rinsed with hot water

1/2 cup cashew pieces

3/4 cup mayonnaise

1 teaspoon curry powder

salt to taste

1/2 teaspoon white pepper

12 romaine leaves

2 ripe papayas, peeled, seeded and cut into
   halves lengthwise

4 pineapple slices

4 clusters red seedless grapes

1 cup strawberries

paprika to taste

Reserve four parsley sprigs for garnish and chop the remaining parsley. Combine the chopped parsley with the chicken, celery, green onions, raisins and cashews in a large bowl. Add the mayonnaise, curry powder, salt and white pepper and toss to mix well. Chill in the refrigerator.

Arrange three romaine lettuce leaves on each of four serving plates and place one papaya half in the center of each plate. Fill the center of each papaya half with the chicken salad. Arrange the pineapple, grapes and strawberries around the papaya on the plates. Sprinkle with paprika and garnish with the reserved parsley sprigs.

Serves 4

This recipe is courtesy of Cedar Creek Inn, a restaurant in San Juan Caspistrano. Appreciation is extended to Cedar Creek Inn for helping to underwrite the photographs in this book.

The Bells are Ringing
A CALL TO TABLE

El Adobe Restaurant

San Juan Capistrano is fortunate to have a prominent historic adobe structure housing one of the town's oldest restaurants, the El Adobe. The building was originally two separate structures. One was the home of Chavito Yorba, a descendant of Jose Antonio Yorba, who traveled with the Portola Expedition. The present-day Fiesta Room was built in 1810 for use as a stage depot, later as a trading post, and finally as a court of justice. Prisoners were kept in the cellar that is used for wine today. In the 1812 earthquake that destroyed the mission church, the adobe Yorba home was used as a hospital.

continued ➤

El Adobe Taco Salad

thinly sliced lettuce

finely chopped tomatoes

shredded Cheddar and Monterey
  Jack cheese

crisply fried narrow corn
  tortilla strips

chopped grilled chicken

chopped green onions

sour cream

guacamole

El Adobe Salsa Borracha (below)

Place the lettuce in a bowl. Sprinkle tomatoes, cheese, tortilla strips, grilled chicken and green onions in concentric circles over the lettuce. Top with scoops of sour cream and guacamole and serve with El Adobe Salsa Borracha to pour over the salad at serving time. The salad will form its own dressing as it is tossed.

Note: This salad is somewhat like a traditional Cobb salad, but with a Mexican twist. It is easy to make at home and is delicious for a luncheon or light summer dinner. It is a favorite at Guild luncheons.

Makes a variable amount

El Adobe Salsa Borracha

3 tomatoes, chopped

3 jalapeño chiles, chopped

1/2 onion, chopped

1/2 bunch cilantro, chopped

juice of 1 1/2 limes

1/2 tablespoon Worcestershire
  sauce

1 teaspoon oregano

1/2 teaspoon salt

Combine the tomatoes, jalapeños, onion and cilantro in a bowl. Add the lime juice, Worcestershire sauce, oregano and salt and mix well.

Makes 4 cups

Crisp Greens with Baked Peppers and Goat Cheese

2 or 3 red bell peppers
1 tablespoon olive oil
1/2 cup crumbled goat cheese
1/3 cup sour cream
1 egg yolk
1/4 teaspoon Tabasco sauce
1/4 teaspoon Worcestershire sauce
salt and pepper to taste
mixed greens

Preheat the oven to 425 degrees. Line a roasting pan with crumpled foil to prevent the bell peppers from rolling around. Cut the bell peppers lengthwise into halves or quarters, depending on their size, discarding the seeds and membranes. Brush lightly with olive oil and arrange skin side down in the prepared pan.

Combine the goat cheese, sour cream, egg yolk, Tabasco sauce, Worcestershire sauce, salt and pepper in a bowl and mix with a fork. Spoon into the cavities of the peppers. Bake for 15 to 20 minutes or until lightly puffed and brown. Serve warm over mixed greens.

Serves 4

The two adobe structures were joined in 1910 to form the El Adobe de Capistrano Restaurant, still famed today for its old California and Mexican cuisine. It was a favorite dining spot of President Richard Nixon and his family when visiting the Western White House in San Clemente, California.
The present owner is Richard O'Neill, whose family came from Ireland in 1882 and oversees and owns Rancho Mission Viejo. The site, along with Mission San Juan Capistrano and numerous others, is listed in the National Inventory of Historic and Cultural Landmarks.

Appreciation is extended
to El Adobe Restaurant for
helping to underwrite
the photographs in this book.

The Bells are Ringing
A CALL TO TABLE

Wilted Greens with Bacon and Garlic Vinaigrette

3 slices bacon, cut crosswise into strips

1 tablespoon olive oil

1 large garlic clove, crushed

2 tablespoons red wine vinegar

16 ounces mixed salad greens or baby
   spinach leaves

Cook the bacon in a skillet until crisp and brown. Remove, drain and crumble the bacon, reserving the drippings in the skillet. Add the olive oil and garlic to the reserved drippings and sauté until the garlic is tender but not brown. Add the vinegar and bring to a boil. Pour the warm dressing over the salad greens in a salad bowl and add the crumbled bacon. Toss to coat well.

Serves 4

Salad Supreme

1 cup French salad dressing

1 cup mayonnaise

1 tablespoon cream or heavy cream

1 teaspoon anchovy paste

1 garlic clove, peeled

1 small cucumber, peeled

1 head romaine, torn

1 head iceberg lettuce, chopped

2 cups baby spinach leaves

1/2 green bell pepper, sliced into thin rounds

1/2 red bell pepper, sliced into thin rounds

1 cup cherry tomatoes, cut into halves

1/2 red onion, thinly sliced

1/2 cup crumbled goat cheese

2 slices bacon, chopped and crisp-cooked

Process the salad dressing, mayonnaise, cream, anchovy paste and garlic in a blender until smooth. Cut the cucumber into halves lengthwise. Remove the seeds and cut the cucumber into thin slices. Combine the cucumber, romaine, iceberg lettuce, spinach, bell peppers, tomatoes, onion, goat cheese and bacon in a large bowl and toss to mix. Add the dressing and toss to coat.

Serves 8 to 10

The Bells are Ringing
A CALL TO TABLE

Greek Salad with Garlic Dressing

Garlic Dressing

> 6 tablespoons extra-virgin olive oil
>
> 2 tablespoons fresh lemon juice
>
> 2 teaspoons red wine vinegar
>
> 2 garlic cloves, finely chopped or minced
>
> 3/4 teaspoon oregano
>
> 1/2 teaspoon thyme
>
> 1/2 teaspoon freshly ground pepper

Salad

> 1 large head romaine
>
> 12 ounces cherry tomatoes, whole or
>
>   cut into halves (about 1 1/2 cups)
>
> 1/2 cup chopped seeded peeled cucumber
>
> 1/2 sweet red onion, thinly sliced
>
> 1/2 cup brine-cured black olives,
>
>   coarsely chopped
>
> 3/4 cup crumbled feta cheese
>
> salt to taste (optional)

For the dressing, combine the olive oil, lemon juice and vinegar in a small bowl. Add the garlic, oregano, thyme and pepper and whisk until smooth. Let stand at room temperature for up to 3 hours. Whisk again at serving time.

For the salad, reserve several of the romaine leaves to line the salad bowl. Tear the remaining leaves into bite-size pieces. Combine the torn romaine with the tomatoes, cucumber, onion and black olives in a salad bowl lined with the reserved lettuce leaves. Add the dressing and toss to coat well. Sprinkle with the feta cheese and season with salt if needed.

Serves 6

Favorite Spinach Salad

Horseradish Poppy Seed Dressing

1 cup vegetable oil

1/3 cup cider vinegar

1 tablespoon onion juice or grated onion

1 teaspoon Dijon mustard

3/4 cup cottage cheese

6 tablespoons horseradish

1/4 cup sugar

1 teaspoon poppy seeds

1 teaspoon salt

Salad

2 pounds spinach, thoroughly washed and torn

8 ounces bacon, crisp-cooked and crumbled

2 hard-cooked eggs, chopped

1 pound fresh mushrooms, sliced

1/2 cup chopped pecans

For the dressing, combine the oil, vinegar, onion juice and Dijon mustard in a 1-quart jar or blender. Add the cottage cheese, horseradish, sugar, poppy seeds and salt and shake or process until smooth; using a blender will produce a creamier dressing.

For the salad, combine the spinach, bacon, eggs, mushrooms and pecans in a large salad bowl. Add the desired amount of dressing and toss lightly to coat well.

Note: The dressing recipe will make more dressing than is needed. Store any unused dressing, covered, in the refrigerator.

Serves 6 to 8

Avocado and Citrus Salad with Poppy Seed Dressing

Poppy Seed Dressing

> 5 tablespoons cider vinegar
>
> 1/3 cup sugar
>
> 1 teaspoon dry mustard
>
> 1 teaspoon salt
>
> 1 cup olive oil or canola oil
>
> 1 1/2 teaspoons drained grated onion
>
> 2 1/2 teaspoons poppy seeds

Salad

> Boston lettuce leaves, washed and chilled
>
> 2 ripe avocados, cut lengthwise into 1/4-inch slices
>
> 2 large red grapefruit or oranges, separated into sections

For the dressing, combine the vinegar, sugar, dry mustard and salt in a bowl. Add the olive oil gradually, beating until well mixed. Add the onion and then the poppy seeds and mix well. Mix well again at serving time.

For the salad, line salad plates with lettuce leaves. Arrange the avocado and grapefruit on the prepared plate. Drizzle with the dressing.

Serves 4 to 6

Green Salad with Oranges, Pecans and Cranberry Dressing

Cranberry Dressing

> 1¹/₄ cups orange juice
>
> 6 tablespoons dried cranberries
>
> ¹/₄ cup olive oil
>
> 2 tablespoons red wine vinegar or
>   fruit-flavored vinegar
>
> 1 teaspoon sugar
>
> 1 tablespoon grated orange zest
>
> salt and pepper to taste

Salad

> 6 cups torn romaine and/or baby spinach
>
> 3 oranges, separated into sections
>
> 1 cup toasted pecans

For the dressing, combine the orange juice with the cranberries in a 2-cup microwave-safe glass measuring cup. Microwave until the orange juice is simmering. Let stand for 30 minutes; drain.

Combine the olive oil, vinegar, sugar and orange zest in a bowl. Add the cranberries and season with salt and pepper. Store in the refrigerator until needed and bring to room temperature before serving.

For the salad, place the romaine in a large salad bowl. Add the dressing and toss to coat well. Spoon onto serving plates and top with the orange sections and pecans.

Serves 6

Mission Salad with Champagne Vinaigrette

Champagne Vinaigrette

> 1 tablespoon minced shallot
>
> 1 teaspoon Dijon mustard
>
> 2 tablespoons champagne vinegar
>
> 1/4 cup plus 2 tablespoons canola oil or vegetable oil
>
>> (2 tablespoons macadamia nut oil can be subsituted
>>
>> for 2 tablespoons of the canola oil or vegetable oil)
>
> salt and pepper to taste

Salad

> 3 large bunches watercress with stems removed, or mixed greens
>
> salt and pepper to taste
>
> 2 pears, peeled, cored and thinly sliced
>
> 1 ounce Parmesan cheese, thinly shaved
>
> 1/2 cup toasted walnuts, coarsely chopped

For the vinaigrette, combine the shallot, Dijon mustard and vinegar in a bowl and whisk to mix well. Whisk in the canola oil gradually and season with salt and pepper.

For the salad, combine the watercress and dressing in a salad bowl. Season with salt and pepper and toss to coat well. Add the pears and Parmesan cheese and toss lightly. Sprinkle with the walnuts before serving.

Serves 6

Citrus and Red Onion Salad

Citrus Dressing

 5 tablespoons olive oil

 3 tablespoons fresh orange juice

 2 tablespoons fresh lemon juice

 1 teaspoon sugar

 1/4 teaspoon salt

 1/4 teaspoon ground ginger

 pinch of pepper

Salad

 3 to 4 cups assorted salad greens such as romaine,
   torn into bite-size pieces

 2 sweet red onions, very thinly sliced

 3 large oranges, peeled, seeded and thinly sliced

 2 pink grapefruit, peeled, seeded and separated into sections

For the dressing, whisk the olive oil, orange juice, lemon juice, sugar, salt, ginger and pepper in a bowl.
For the salad, place the salad greens in a shallow salad bowl. Add half the dressing and toss to coat. Arrange the red onions, oranges and grapefruit on top of the salad greens. Drizzle the remaining salad dressing over the top of the salad.

Serves 4 to 6

Pear and Endive Salad

Light Vinaigrette

    1/2 cup olive oil

    1 teaspoon salt

    dash of freshly ground pepper

    2 teaspoons Dijon mustard

    1 teaspoon prepared horseradish

    2 teaspoons white balsamic vinegar

Salad

    3 heads endive

    2 large pears, cut into thin slices

    1 small onion, thinly sliced

    1/2 cup crumbled feta cheese

For the vinaigrette, whisk the olive oil, salt, pepper, Dijon mustard, horseradish and balsamic vinegar together in a bowl.

For the salad, cut out the small core at the base of the endive. Chop the endive into large pieces. Combine the endive, pears, onion and feta cheese in a salad bowl and toss to mix. Place on salad plates and serve the vinaigrette on the side or drizzle over each salad.

Note: You may use green apples instead of the pears.

Serves 4 to 6

Cranberry and Pineapple Salad

2 (3-ounce) packages cranberry gelatin or
   raspberry gelatin
1¹/₂ cups boiling water
2 (16-ounce) cans whole cranberry sauce

1 (16-ounce) can crushed pineapple
1 cup chopped walnuts
¹/₂ cup chopped celery
1 cup sour cream

Combine the gelatin with the boiling water in a large bowl, stirring for 2 minutes or until the gelatin is completely dissolved. Add the cranberry sauce, pineapple, walnuts and celery and mix well. Spoon half the gelatin into a 9×13-inch dish and chill until partially set. Spread the sour cream over the chilled layer and spoon the remaining gelatin mixture carefully over the sour cream. Chill for 8 hours or longer. Cut into squares to serve.

Serves 6

Divine Fruit Salad Platter

1 cup vegetable oil
¹/₄ cup each pineapple juice and lemon juice
¹/₄ cup sugar
¹/₂ teaspoon salt
lettuce leaves
3 firm ripe bananas
lemon juice

2 lemons, cut into 6 to 8 wedges each
6 small wedges watermelon
6 wedges cantaloupe or honeydew melon
3 kiwifruit, sliced
1 small pineapple, cut into spears
2 cups whole strawberries
1 cup blueberries or raspberries

Process the oil, pineapple juice, lemon juice, sugar and salt in a blender until combined. Pour in a serving bowl and chill in the refrigerator. Line a platter with lettuce leaves. Cut the bananas into quarters and dip in lemon juice to prevent discoloration. Arrange the lemon wedges around the edge of the platter. Arrange the remaining fruit on the platter. Stir the dressing and serve with the fruit.

Serves 6 to 8

Jalapeño and Pineapple Coleslaw

1 cup mayonnaise

1 cup sour cream or plain yogurt

1¹/2 tablespoons Dijon mustard

2 tablespoons fresh lemon juice

3 pickled jalapeño chiles, stemmed and minced

3 tablespoons sugar

¹/2 teaspoon salt

1 cabbage, chopped (about 8 cups)

1 (16-ounce) can pineapple tidbits, or 2 cups chopped fresh pineapple

3 green onions, chopped

Whisk the mayonnaise, sour cream, Dijon mustard, lemon juice, jalapeños, sugar and salt together in a large bowl. Stir in the cabbage and pineapple. Chill, covered, for 1 to 24 hours. Add the chopped green onions and adjust the seasonings to taste just before serving.

Serves 8

Scene from annual "Swallows Parade," downtown San Juan Capistrano, California

Life on the Rancho

Life on the rancho was simple but challenging. Food was abundant, hospitality was generous, manners were elegant, and recreation and leisure were highly valued, with regular events featuring music and dancing. The annual cattle roundup or rodeo took place over several days and was great cause for celebration. Despite the hard work, it was an opportunity to delight in family, friends, contests of riding skill, and sumptuous feasts. Typical fare included all types of barbecued meats, tamales, salsa, tortillas, beans, and rice.

The Bells are Ringing
A CALL TO TABLE

Los Vaqueros

Los vaqueros were the proficient horsemen of the ranchos, known for their riding skills and competent use of lariats or riatas in herding cattle.

When following the herds, the vaqueros required food that kept well despite the lack of proper storage or refrigeration, and dried beef was ideal for the trail. It could be eaten out of the hand as jerky or shredded and cooked in a stew over the open campfire.

Green Nugget Salad

1 (10-ounce) package frozen green peas,
    thawed and drained
1/2 cup mayonnaise
1/2 cup sour cream
3 tablespoons grated onion
1/2 cup salted Spanish peanuts
tomato aspic ring or sliced tomatoes
lettuce leaves (optional)

Combine the uncooked peas with the mayonnaise, sour cream, onion and peanuts in a bowl and mix well. Chill for 8 hours or longer to develop the flavors. Serve in a tomato aspic ring or spooned onto sliced tomatoes on a bed of lettuce leaves.

Serves 4 to 6

The Blessing by Bill Owens

Asparagus Basil Salad

8 ounces asparagus, trimmed

1 tablespoon finely chopped pimento

1/4 cup chopped fresh basil leaves

2 tablespoons red wine vinegar

2 tablespoons olive oil

1/2 teaspoon dried tarragon

Salt and pepper to taste

1 hard-cooked egg, minced

Cook the asparagus in boiling water until just tender. Plunge immediately into ice water to stop the cooking process. Drain and chill in the refrigerator. Place the chilled asparagus in a shallow serving bowl. Sprinkle with the pimento and basil. Whisk the vinegar, olive oil, tarragon, salt and pepper in a bowl. Pour over the asparagus and top with the minced egg.

Serves 4

Broccoli Salad

5 broccoli crowns, coarsely chopped

12 slices bacon, crisp-cooked and crumbled

1/2 cup raisins

1/2 cup sunflower seeds

1/2 cup chopped sweet red onion

1 cup mayonnaise

2 tablespoons red wine vinegar

1/3 cup sugar

Combine the broccoli, bacon, raisins, sunflower seeds and red onion in a bowl and toss to mix. Whisk the mayonnaise, vinegar and sugar in a bowl until blended. Pour over the broccoli mixture and toss to mix well. Chill for several hours before serving.

Serves 6 to 8

Avocado Dressing

1 ripe avocado, mashed
1/2 cup sour cream
1/3 cup olive oil
1 tablespoon lemon juice
1 garlic clove, crushed

1/2 teaspoon sugar
1/4 teaspoon hot red pepper sauce
1/2 teaspoon chili powder
1/4 teaspoon salt

Combine the avocado, sour cream, olive oil and lemon juice in a blender. Add the garlic, sugar, hot sauce, chili powder and salt and process until smooth. Store in a covered container in the refrigerator. Serve over chilled greens.

Makes 2 cups

Blue Cheese Dressing

8 ounces cream cheese, softened
1/2 cup crumbled blue cheese
1 cup mayonnaise

1 cup sour cream
1/4 cup cider vinegar
1 garlic clove, crushed

Combine the cream cheese, blue cheese, mayonnaise, sour cream, vinegar and garlic in a blender and process until smooth. Store in an airtight container in the refrigerator. Shake before serving.

Note: This can also be served as a dip. To reduce the fat content, use low-fat products.

Makes 3 to 4 cups

Easy Salad Dressing

1 (10-ounce) can tomato soup
1/2 cup cider vinegar
3/4 cup extra-virgin olive oil
1 garlic clove, crushed

2 tablespoons sugar
1/8 teaspoon paprika
1/8 teaspoon red pepper flakes
1/8 teaspoon salt

Combine the soup, vinegar, olive oil, garlic, sugar, paprika, red pepper flakes and salt in a jar and shake to mix well. Chill in the refrigerator. Serve over chilled greens.

Makes 3 cups

Green Goddess Salad Dressing

1 cup mayonnaise
1/2 cup sour cream
2 tablespoons tarragon vinegar
1/2 teaspoon lemon juice
1 tablespoon anchovy paste
1 garlic clove, crushed

2 tablespoons finely chopped
    green onions with tops
1/8 teaspoon pepper
2 or 3 drops of green
    food coloring

Whisk together the mayonnaise, sour cream, vinegar, lemon juice and anchovy paste in a bowl. Add the garlic, green onions, pepper and food coloring and mix well. Chill for 2 to 3 hours.

Makes 1 2/3 cups

President Abraham Lincoln

One month before his assassination in 1865, President Abraham Lincoln signed documents decreeing that control of California's mission sites be returned to the Catholic Church. The Mission celebrates President Lincoln's unique legacy and role in its history through its Rancho Room exhibit and the annual Lincoln Day Celebration. On the day of the celebration the priceless original document that returned its control to the Church and bears Lincoln's signature is put on public display under security's careful watch.

Seafood Louis Dressing

2 cups mayonnaise

1 1/2 cups chili sauce

2 teaspoons fresh lemon juice

1 teaspoon horseradish

1 teaspoon Worcestershire sauce

1 cup finely chopped dill pickle, or

   1/4 cup pickle relish

1 hard-cooked egg, chopped

3 tablespoons finely chopped parsley

capers to taste

Combine the mayonnaise, chili sauce, lemon juice, horseradish and Worcestershire sauce in a medium bowl. Add the pickle, egg, parsley and capers and mix well. Spoon into a covered 1 1/2-quart jar and store in the refrigerator.

Makes 4 cups

Herb Vinaigrette

2 cups olive oil

3/4 cup balsamic vinegar

1 tablespoon minced garlic

1 tablespoon minced shallots

1 tablespoon minced chives

1 tablespoon minced fresh basil

1/2 teaspoon sugar

1 (3-ounce) jar capers, drained (optional)

1/2 teaspoon salt

1/4 teaspoon pepper

Combine the olive oil and balsamic vinegar in a container with a lid. Add the garlic, shallots, chives, basil, sugar, capers, salt and pepper. Store in the refrigerator. Shake well before serving.

Makes 3 cups

Chunky Monkey Bars

1 large package brownie mix
8 ounces chocolate chips
3/4 cup chopped roasted peanuts
1/2 cup honey
1/4 cup creamy peanut butter

Preheat the oven using the brownie mix package directions. Prepare and bake the brownie mix in a greased 9×13-inch baking dish, using the directions for cake-like brownies. Remove from the oven and sprinkle immediately with the chocolate chips and peanuts.

Combine the honey and peanut butter in a saucepan. Heat over low heat until smooth and heated through. Pour over the prepared layers and let stand until cool. Chill slightly for ease of cutting.

Makes 1 dozen

Ooey-Gooey Peanut Butter Cookies

1¹/₂ cups sugar

1¹/₂ cups light corn syrup

1¹/₂ cups creamy or chunky peanut butter

1 cup chocolate chips

4¹/₂ cups plain or cocoa crisp rice cereal

Combine the sugar and corn syrup in a medium saucepan and bring to a full boil. Pour into a large heatproof bowl and add the peanut butter, chocolate chips and cereal; mix well. Drop by tablespoonfuls onto a waxed paper-lined tray and let stand until firm.

Makes 2 dozen

Sugar Cookies

3 1/2 cups sifted all-purpose flour
1 teaspoon baking soda
2 teaspoons cream of tartar
1/2 teaspoon salt
1 cup (2 sticks) butter, softened
1 teaspoon vanilla extract
1 1/2 cups sugar
3 eggs

Sift the flour, baking soda, cream of tartar and salt together. Cream the butter with the vanilla in a mixing bowl until light. Add the sugar gradually, beating until fluffy. Beat in the eggs one at a time. Add the dry ingredients gradually, mixing to form a dough. Chill for 3 to 4 hours.

Preheat the oven to 375 degrees. Roll the dough 1/8 to 1/4 inch thick on a floured surface. Cut into the desired shapes and place widely separated on ungreased or baking parchment-lined cookie sheets. Bake for 6 to 8 minutes or until light golden brown. Cool slightly on the cookie sheets and remove to a wire rack to cool completely.

Note: You can make cookies to hang on a tree by piercing a hole with a straw or wooden pick before baking. You can also decorate the cookies with colored sugar before baking or while still warm, or glaze with confectioners' sugar glaze when cool.

Makes about 8 dozen

California Statehood and the Ranchos

At the end of the Mexican-American War, and with the onset of the Gold Rush, confusion reigned over the fate of the ranchos. California statehood was approved on September 9, 1850.

Then, in accordance with the California Land Claims Act, ranchos were confiscated if owners could not produce official deeds of ownership. Heavy rains, then drought, followed by a smallpox epidemic caused further havoc in the area. Eventually, combined acts of man and nature changed California rancho life forever. Weathered and worn, the old Mission still stood nobly in San Juan Capistrano.

Ice Cream Crunch Cake

1 cup (6 ounces) chocolate chips
2/3 cup creamy peanut butter
6 cups crisp rice cereal

1 gallon vanilla ice cream, softened

Combine the chocolate chips and peanut butter in a large saucepan. Heat over low heat until the chips melt, stirring to mix well. Stir in the cereal until well coated. Spread on a baking sheet and let stand until cool. Break the mixture into small pieces.

Reserve 1 cup of the chocolate mixture and stir the remaining into the softened ice cream in a bowl. Spread in a 10-inch springform pan and sprinkle the reserved chocolate mixture over the top. Freeze until firm. Garnish servings with whipped cream or whipped topping and strawberries.

Serves 12

Pumpkin Upside-Down Cake

1 (29-ounce) can pumpkin
1 1/4 cups sugar
1 (12-ounce) can evaporated milk
3 eggs, beaten
2 teaspoons ground cinnamon
1 teaspoon grated nutmeg

1/2 teaspoon ground ginger
1 (2-layer) package yellow cake mix
1 cup chopped walnuts
1/2 to 1 cup (1 to 2 sticks) butter, melted

Preheat the oven to 350 degrees. Combine the pumpkin, sugar, evaporated milk, eggs, cinnamon, nutmeg and ginger in a bowl and mix well. Spoon into a greased 9×13-inch cake pan.

Sprinkle the cake mix and then the walnuts over the pumpkin mixture; drizzle with the butter to moisten. Bake for 1 hour. Serve warm with whipped cream.

Serves 10 to 12

Tea Sandwiches

peanut butter
jelly
20 slices bread
8 ounces cream cheese, softened
2 cucumbers, thinly sliced
chopped parsley (optional)

Spread peanut butter and jelly on five slices of the bread and top each with another slice of the bread. Spread cream cheese on five slices of bread. Arrange the cucumber slices and parsley over the cream cheese and top with the remaining five slices of bread. Trim the crusts from the sandwiches and cut each into three fingers. Arrange on a platter.

Makes 30

Pastry-Rolled Hot Dogs

1 refrigerator pie pastry
1 (5-ounce) can Vienna sausages

Preheat the oven to 350 degrees. Roll the pie pastry on a floured surface and cut into strips 3/4 inch wide. Place a sausage on each strip and roll the pastry around each sausage three times. Place on a baking sheet and bake for 10 to 12 minutes or until golden brown.

Note: Children love to make and eat these treats. They can also wrap cheese cubes in the pastry or cut out desired shapes and sprinkle them with cinnamon-sugar.

Makes 8

A Call to Dinner

Savor the Rewards of the Day's Labor

The Mission's Soldiers Barracks, where our dinner selections are displayed, shows the type of accommodations provided for the Spanish soldiers who accompanied the padres and protected them on their expedition to establish Mission San Juan Capistrano. These soldiers were known as the "Leather Jackets" due to the heavy deer-hide vests they wore to protect them from arrows. Up to four or five stayed on at a time to protect the Mission after its founding, and a few of their direct descendants still live in San Juan Capistrano.

Now we come to the dinner table, celebrating the day and looking forward to tomorrow. Here you will find recipes for hearty and satisfying meals. Add to that a few more historical snapshots of this final period from President Lincoln's decree, 1865 to the present.

Barbecued Beef Brisket

Brisket

  1 (4$\frac{1}{2}$- to 5$\frac{1}{2}$-pound) beef brisket

  2 (14-ounce) cans beef broth

  seasoned salt to taste

  $\frac{1}{2}$ to 1 teaspoon garlic powder

  2 to 3 teaspoons liquid smoke

Barbecue Sauce

  1 onion, chopped

  1 tablespoon butter

  1 cup drippings reserved from the brisket, degreased

  $\frac{1}{2}$ cup ketchup

  2 tablespoons Worcestershire sauce

  2 tablespoons red wine vinegar

  2 teaspoons liquid smoke

  $\frac{1}{2}$ cup packed brown sugar

  1 teaspoon dry mustard

  1 teaspoon salt

  $\frac{1}{2}$ teaspoon pepper

For the brisket, preheat the oven to 250 degrees. Sear the brisket on all sides in a large nonstick skillet. Remove to a heavy roasting pan and add the beef broth, seasoned salt and garlic powder. Rub with the liquid smoke. Roast for 2 hours. Pour off 1 cup of the pan drippings for the barbecue sauce. Return the brisket to the oven and roast for 2$\frac{1}{2}$ to 3$\frac{1}{2}$ hours longer, or for a total of 1 hour per pound.

For the sauce, sauté the onion in the butter in a heavy saucepan for 3 minutes. Add the reserved pan drippings, ketchup, Worcestershire sauce, vinegar, liquid smoke, brown sugar, dry mustard, salt and pepper. Mix well and simmer for 2 hours.

To finish, increase the oven temperature to 325 degrees. Drain the brisket and degrease the cooking liquid from the brisket to thin the sauce if needed. Let the brisket stand at room temperature for 1 hour. Slice as thinly as possible across the grain and place in a baking dish. Pour the barbecue sauce over the brisket. Bake, covered, for 1 hour or until heated through, adding some of the reserved cooking liquid if needed for the desired consistency. Serve as part of a barbecue buffet with rolls, baked beans and coleslaw.

Serves 6

Easy Beef Brisket

1 (4-pound) beef brisket
1 (10-ounce) can French onion soup
1/2 cup sherry
1 tablespoon salt

1 tablespoon pepper
1 garlic clove, crushed
1 bay leaf

Preheat the oven to 325 degrees. Place the brisket fatty side up in a 9×13-inch baking pan. Pour the soup and sherry over the brisket. Season with the salt, pepper, garlic and bay leaf. Bake for 3 1/2 to 4 hours or until tender. Remove the brisket from the baking pan to a cutting board and let stand for 5 to 10 minutes. Slice as thinly as possible across the grain and return to the juices in the baking pan. Return to the oven until ready to serve. Remove the sliced brisket to a large platter, discarding the bay leaf and pouring any remaining juice over the top. Garnish with parsley and sliced tomatoes. Serve with garlic mashed potatoes.

Serves 6

Beef Tenderloin with Cognac Mustard Sauce

Tenderloin

1 (4-pound) beef tenderloin
1 tablespoon olive oil
1 teaspoon coarse salt
2 teaspoons freshly ground pepper

Cognac Mustard Sauce

1/2 cup Dijon mustard
1/4 cup mayonnaise
1/4 cup sour cream
2 tablespoons cognac

For the tenderloin, preheat the oven to 425 degrees. Rub the tenderloin with the olive oil, salt and pepper. Place on a rack in a roasting pan and insert a meat thermometer into the thickest portion. Roast for 45 to 60 minutes, or to 145 degrees for medium-rare or 160 degrees for medium. Let stand, covered with foil, for 10 minutes before slicing.

For the sauce, combine the Dijon mustard, mayonnaise, sour cream and cognac in a saucepan and mix well. Heat just until warmed through. Serve with the sliced tenderloin.

Serves 8

The Bells are Ringing
A CALL TO TABLE

Perfect-Every-Time Standing Rib Roast

1 standing prime rib roast
all-purpose flour
salt and pepper to taste

Let the roast stand at room temperature for 2 to 4 hours before roasting. Preheat the oven to 500 degrees. Place the roast fat side up in a shallow roasting pan. Rub with flour and season with salt and pepper. Roast for 5 minutes per pound. Turn off the oven and let the roast stand in the closed oven for about two hours; do not open the oven.

Serves a variable amount

Bohemian Flank Steak

1 (1¹/2-pound) flank steak
¹/2 cup olive oil
¹/2 cup garlic-flavored red wine vinegar
2 tablespoons red wine

2 tablespoons finely chopped green chiles
2 teaspoons seasoned salt
¹/2 teaspoon Java pepper
1 small onion, sliced and separated into rings

Place the flank steak in a shallow baking dish. Combine the olive oil, vinegar, wine, green chiles, seasoned salt and Java pepper in a bowl; mix well. Pour over the steak. Top with the onion, spooning some of the marinade over the rings. Marinate, covered, in the refrigerator for 8 hours or longer.

Let the steak stand at room temperature for 30 minutes. Preheat the broiler. Remove the steak to a rack in a very shallow broiling pan, reserving the marinade and onion rings. Broil 3 inches from the heat source for 5 minutes on each side for rare, basting several times with the reserved marinade. About 2 minutes before the steak is done, spoon the reserved onion rings over the steak and broil until the onion is tender. Slice the steak very thin on the diagonal and serve the onion rings over the slices.

Serves 4

*The Bells are Ringing*
A CALL TO TABLE

Mexican Steak with Cilantro Yogurt Sauce

Cilantro Yogurt Sauce

1/2 cup low-fat plain yogurt

1/4 cup light mayonnaise

1 teaspoon lime juice

1/4 teaspoon grated lime zest

1/3 cup chopped fresh cilantro

1/8 teaspoon salt

Steak

3 tablespoons chili powder

1 teaspoon ground coriander

1 teaspoon cumin

3/4 teaspoon salt

1 (11/4-pound) flank steak

1 large garlic clove, cut into halves lengthwise

10 to 12 (6- to 7-inch) flour tortillas, warmed

3 cups thinly sliced romaine

For the sauce, combine the yogurt, mayonnaise, lime juice, lime zest, cilantro and salt in a bowl; mix well and set aside.

For the steak, preheat the grill. Mix the chili powder, coriander, cumin and salt in a small bowl. Rub both sides of the steak with the garlic and then with the chili powder mixture. Grill the steak for 4 minutes on each side for rare, or to the desired degree of doneness. Let stand for 5 minutes and slice thinly across the grain. Serve in the tortillas with the sauce and sliced romaine.

Serves 4 to 6

The Bells are Ringing
A CALL TO TABLE

Beef Stew with Red Wine and Cream

4 pounds beef chuck, trimmed and cut into
   1¹/2-inch cubes
3 ribs celery, coarsely chopped
2 large carrots, coarsely chopped
2 onions, coarsely chopped
2 cups merlot or other dry red wine
2 bay leaves
1 tablespoon chopped fresh rosemary
2 tablespoons chopped fresh thyme

1 tablespoon pink peppercorns
¹/4 cup olive oil
¹/4 cup all-purpose flour
¹/4 cup red wine vinegar
¹/4 cup tomato paste
4 cups chicken broth or beef broth
¹/4 cup red currant jelly
¹/2 cup cream or heavy cream
salt and pepper to taste

Combine the beef with the celery, carrots and onions in a large bowl. Add the wine, bay leaves, rosemary, thyme and peppercorns; toss to coat evenly. Marinate, covered, in the refrigerator for 8 hours or longer, stirring several times.

Drain the beef and vegetables in a colander set over a bowl, reserving the marinade. Heat half the olive oil in a large heavy saucepan over medium-high heat. Add half the beef and cook for 5 minutes or until light brown on all sides; remove to a bowl and repeat with the remaining olive oil and beef. Add the vegetables to the pan drippings and cook for 2 minutes. Return the beef to the saucepan.

Stir in the flour and cook for 2 minutes. Add the vinegar, stirring constantly to stir up any browned bits from the bottom of the pan. Add the reserved marinade and tomato paste. Simmer for 2 minutes, stirring constantly. Stir in the chicken broth and jelly; season with salt and pepper. Bring to a boil and reduce the heat to low. Simmer for 2 to 2¹/2 hours or until the beef is very tender, stirring occasionally.

Drain the mixture in a colander set over a bowl. Remove the beef to a platter. Press the solids in the colander to remove as much liquid as possible, discarding the remaining solids. Pour the liquid back into the saucepan and add the beef. Stir in the cream and bring just to a simmer. Season with salt and pepper and garnish with sprigs of fresh thyme.

Serves 6

Beef and Onion Stew

4 ounces lean bacon, chopped

1 tablespoon butter

20 small boiling onions, peeled

1 large garlic clove, minced

2 pounds boneless chuck, cut
    into 1¹/₂-inch cubes

1 tablespoon (or more) olive oil

2 teaspoons all-purpose flour

1 to 2 teaspoons salt, or to taste

¹/₂ teaspoon freshly
    ground pepper

12 ounces dark beer

1 tablespoon lemon juice

¹/₄ cup chopped fresh parsley

Place the bacon in a heatproof bowl and cover with boiling water. Let stand for 1 minute; drain. Cook the bacon and butter in a large skillet over medium heat until the bacon just begins to brown. Add the onions and garlic and cook until golden brown, stirring frequently. Spoon into a Dutch oven or ovenproof baking dish with a lid. Brown the beef cubes in batches in the olive oil in the skillet over high heat, adding additional olive oil if necessary. Do not crowd the beef in the skillet or it will not brown properly. Add the browned beef to the Dutch oven. Stir in the flour, salt and pepper. Add enough of the beer to barely cover the beef. Bring to a boil over high heat. Reduce the heat and simmer, covered, for 1¹/₂ hours or until the beef is tender, adding more beer if necessary. Adjust the seasonings to taste. Remove from the heat and stir in the lemon juice. Serve with noodles and sprinkle with the parsley.

Serves 6

Carne Seca

Place a beef roast or brisket in a slow-cooker and cook on Low for 12 to 18 hours or until most of the moisture has evaporated and the beef is dry. Shred the beef and combine with 1 chopped small onion, 5 chopped tomatoes, 3 chopped green chiles and 2 minced garlic cloves in a saucepan. Add 1 cup chili Colorado, ¹/₂ teaspoon ground cumin, ¹/₂ teaspoon oregano, and 1 teaspoon salt. Simmer for 1 hour.

Sarducci's Chili

2 pounds ground beef

1¹/2 tablespoons chopped garlic

1 large white onion, chopped

¹/4 cup chopped celery

1 tablespoon chili powder

1 green bell pepper, chopped

1 red bell pepper, chopped

1 yellow bell pepper, chopped

1 jalapeño chile, sliced

2 tomatoes, chopped

1 (20-ounce) can diced tomatoes

1 teaspoon salt

1¹/2 cups chicken stock

1 (20-ounce) can kidney beans

1 (15-ounce) can garbanzo beans

Cook the ground beef with the garlic in a nonstick saucepan until brown and crumbly; drain the ground beef, reserving a small amount of the pan drippings. Add the onion and celery to the reserved drippings in the saucepan and sauté until tender. Add the chili powder and cook for 5 minutes. Add the bell peppers and jalapeño and sauté for 10 minutes. Stir in the fresh tomatoes and undrained canned tomatoes.

Return the ground beef to the saucepan and season with the salt; simmer for 5 minutes. Stir in the chicken stock and simmer for 15 minutes. Add the kidney beans and garbanzo beans and simmer for 5 minutes longer. Serve with corn muffins.

Serves 10

This recipe is courtesy of Sarducci's Capistrano Depot. Appreciation is extended to Sarducci's for helping to underwrite the photographs in this book.

The Bells are Ringing
A CALL TO TABLE

Tamale Pie

Pie

1 1/2 pounds ground beef

2 teaspoons olive oil

1 cup chopped onion

1/2 cup chopped green bell pepper

1 garlic clove, minced or crushed

1 (20-ounce) can diced tomatoes

1 (14-ounce) can whole kernel corn

1 1/2 teaspoons chili powder

1 teaspoon salt

1/4 teaspoon freshly ground pepper

1/2 cup cornmeal

1 cup water

1 (4-ounce) can chopped black olives

Topping

1 1/2 cups milk

2 tablespoons butter

1 teaspoon salt

1/2 cup cornmeal

2 eggs, beaten

1 cup (4 ounces) shredded Cheddar cheese

For the pie, preheat the oven to 375 degrees and spray a large skillet with nonstick cooking spray. Cook the ground beef in the prepared skillet over medium heat until brown and crumbly. Remove the ground beef to a metal colander lined with paper towels to drain. Add the olive oil to the same skillet and add the onion, bell pepper and garlic. Sauté over medium-low heat until the onion is golden brown. Return the ground beef to the skillet and add the tomatoes, corn, chili powder, salt and pepper.

Stir the cornmeal into the water in a small bowl. Add to the ground beef mixture and mix well. Simmer, covered, over low heat for 10 minutes, stirring occasionally. Stir in the olives and spoon into a 3-quart baking dish.

For the topping, scald the milk with the butter and salt in a medium saucepan. Reduce the heat to low and gradually stir in the cornmeal. Cook until thickened, stirring constantly. Remove from the heat and stir 1 cup of the mixture into the eggs; stir the eggs into the hot mixture. Add the cheese and stir until melted. Pour the topping evenly over the pie. Bake for 40 minutes.

Serves 6 to 8

California-Style Veal Piccata

1 egg

2 teaspoons water

2 pounds veal scallops, 1/8 inch thick

1/4 cup all-purpose flour

1/2 teaspoon oregano

1 teaspoon salt

1/2 teaspoon pepper

2 tablespoons (or more) butter

2 tablespoons (or more) olive oil

2 tablespoons minced shallot or other mild onion

1/3 cup dry vermouth or other dry white wine

3/4 cup chicken broth

2 tablespoons fresh lemon juice

salt and pepper to taste

2 tablespoons capers (optional)

chopped fresh parsley (optional)

1 avocado, cut into 8 slices

1 tablespoon fresh lemon juice

thin lemon slices

Beat the egg with the water in a shallow dish. Add the veal slices and let stand in the refrigerator for 1 hour or longer.

Mix the flour, oregano, 1 teaspoon salt and 1/2 teaspoon pepper in a shallow dish. Remove the veal slices from the egg mixture and coat with the flour mixture, shaking to discard any excess flour. Place on a plate lined with waxed paper or baking parchment.

Melt the butter with the olive oil in a 10- to 12-inch covered skillet over medium heat. Add the veal in two or three batches and sauté for 3 minutes on each side or until light brown, adding additional olive oil or butter if necessary. Remove the veal to a plate.

Add the shallot to the drippings in the skillet and sauté over medium heat just until translucent. Stir in the vermouth, broth and 2 tablespoons lemon juice; season with salt and pepper to taste. Cook until the mixture is reduced to a slightly thickened and creamy consistency. Return the veal to the skillet and add the capers. Reduce the heat and simmer for 10 minutes, adding parsley during the last 4 to 5 minutes.

Preheat the oven to 300 degrees. Sprinkle the avocado with 1 tablespoon lemon juice and place in a small baking dish. Bake for 5 minutes.

Remove the veal to a serving plate and arrange the avocado slices and lemon slices around the veal. Spoon the sauce over the top and serve hot.

Serves 4

Veal Saltimbocca

fresh sage leaves
1 pound thinly sliced veal
4 ounces thinly sliced prosciutto
5 tablespoons olive oil
½ cup dry white wine

Layer one or two sage leaves on each slice of veal and top with slices of prosciutto; thread wooden picks through the layers to secure. Heat the olive oil in a skillet over medium-high heat. Add the layers veal side down to the skillet. Sauté until the veal is golden brown and turn. Sauté until the prosciutto is golden brown, taking care not to overcook. Add the wine to the skillet, scraping up any browned bits on the bottom. Cook until the wine evaporates. Remove the veal to a platter and spoon any pan juices over the top. Serve immediately.

Serves 4

The State of the Mission

By the 1890s Mission San Juan Capistrano was little more than a shadow of its former self. Many roofs had caved in, allowing water to erode the original adobe structures. Sheep grazed in the now-open courtyard, and the once abundant gardens and orchards were overrun with vines and weeds.

Sheep Grazing by John Gutzon Borglum

The Bells are Ringing
A CALL TO TABLE

Braised Lamb Shanks with Apricots and Plums

3/4 cup dried pitted plums

1/3 cup port

6 (3/4-pound) lamb shanks

2 garlic cloves, cut into halves

salt and freshly ground pepper to taste

3/4 cup all-purpose flour

1/4 cup (or more) fruity olive oil

1 1/2 cups chopped sweet onions

2 carrots, finely chopped

3/4 cup chopped celery

3 garlic cloves, minced

1 tablespoon minced fresh rosemary

3 tablespoons tomato paste

1 (14-ounce) can chicken broth

1 (14-ounce) can beef broth

3/4 cup merlot

3/4 cup dried apricots

2 bay leaves

Combine the plums with the port in a bowl and let stand to plump. Rub the lamb shanks with the cut sides of the garlic and season with salt and pepper. Spoon the flour in a paper bag. Shake the lamb shanks one at a time in the flour. Heat the olive oil in a large skillet and add the lamb shanks in batches. Cook for 25 to 30 minutes or until brown on all sides, adding additional olive oil if necessary. Remove to a roasting pan large enough to contain the shanks in a single layer.

Preheat the oven to 325 degrees. Add the onions, carrots, celery and minced garlic to the drippings in the skillet and sauté for 5 minutes. Stir in the rosemary. Blend the tomato paste with 2 tablespoons of the chicken broth and add to the skillet with the remaining chicken broth, beef broth and merlot. Season with salt and pepper. Pour over the lamb in the roasting pan. Drain the plums and add the plums, apricots and bay leaves to the pan. Bake, covered, in the center of the oven for 1 hour, basting after after 30 minutes. Turn the shanks over and bake for 1 hour longer, basting after 30 minutes. Arrange the shanks on a platter and keep warm.

Strain the cooking liquid, reserving the fruit and vegetables. Degrease the cooking liquid and return to the pan. Bring to a boil over medium heat and cook until reduced and slightly thickened. Discard the bay leaves and return the fruit and vegetables to the pan; cook just until heated through. Spoon the fruit and vegetables over the lamb and serve the sauce in a gravy boat. Garnish with sprigs of fresh rosemary.

Serves 4 to 6

Grilled Lamb Chops

2 tablespoons red wine vinegar

2 tablespoons honey

2 garlic cloves, minced or crushed

2 tablespoons chopped fresh mint

1¹/₂ teaspoons curry powder

¹/₂ teaspoon dry mustard

¹/₄ cup extra-virgin olive oil

12 small lamb chops, 1¹/₂ to 2 inches
   thick, trimmed

Whisk together the vinegar, honey, garlic, mint, curry powder and dry mustard in a bowl. Add the olive oil gradually, whisking constantly until combined.

Brush the marinade with a pastry brush over all sides for the chops. Place in a covered dish and marinate in the refrigerator for 3 hours or longer. Remove from the refrigerator and let come to room temperature.

Preheat the gas grill to high heat. Grill the lamb until brown on one side. Turn the chops and reduce the heat to medium. Grill for 8 minutes for medium or until done to taste, turning several times. Remove to a warm platter and serve with Party Rice with Toasted Almonds (page 131) and/or Oven-Roasted Tomatoes (page 178).

Serves 6

"Romance" Concert and Dinner Gala, Fall 2004

The Bells are Ringing
A CALL TO TABLE

Lamb Shish Kabobs

Lamb

1/2 cup lime juice

1 large onion, chopped

salt and pepper to taste

1 leg of lamb, boned

Basting Sauce

1/4 teaspoon saffron (optional)

1/2 cup (1 stick) butter, melted

2 tablespoons lime juice

salt and pepper to taste

Kabobs

2 or 3 large green bell peppers

12 small white onions

12 small tomatoes

12 mushrooms

For the lamb, combine the lime juice, onion, salt and pepper in a large bowl. Cut the lamb into 2$1/2$-inch pieces and add to the marinade. Marinate in the refrigerator for 3 to 4 hours, stirring occasionally.

For the basting sauce, blend the saffron with a small amount of water in a bowl. Add the butter, lime juice, salt and pepper.

For the kabobs, preheat the charcoal grill. Cut the bell peppers into 2-inch squares. Parboil the bell peppers and onions until barely tender. Alternate the lamb, onions and bell peppers on long metal skewers. Place the tomatoes and mushrooms on separate skewers.

Grill the lamb kabobs for about 15 minutes, basting with the sauce; do not overcook. Grill the tomatoes and mushrooms until heated through.

Serves 6 to 8

Pork Tenderloin with Dried Fruit

2 pork tenderloins (about 3 pounds)

olive oil

coarse salt and freshly ground pepper to taste

1/2 cup (1 stick) butter, melted

1/2 cup packed brown sugar

1 cup dried apricots

1 cup dried peaches

1 cup dried figs

1 cup dried apples

1 cup dried cranberries or dried cherries

1 cup brandy, cognac or white wine

1 cup water

1/2 teaspoon ground cinnamon

1/4 teaspoon ground allspice

Preheat the oven to 375 degrees. Rub the pork with olive oil, salt and pepper. Place a large sheet of heavy-duty foil in a roasting pan greased with a small amount of olive oil. Place the pork in the pan, bringing the sides of the foil up around the pork without covering it.

Melt the butter in a skillet and stir in the brown sugar. Add the apricots, peaches, figs, apples and cranberries and sauté for 5 minutes. Stir in the brandy, water, cinnamon and allspice. Simmer for 5 minutes. Pour over the pork, taking care to keep everything inside the foil.

Roast for 20 minutes. Turn the pork over and spoon the fruit over the top. Roast for 20 minutes longer. Remove the pork to a serving platter and spoon the fruit and cooking juices around and over the pork.

Serves 6 to 8

Pork Loin with Fresh Peaches

1 to 2 tablespoons olive oil
1 teaspoon salt
3 garlic cloves, crushed
leaves of 2 sprigs fresh rosemary
leaves of 3 sprigs fresh thyme
1 teaspoon salt
1 (3^1/$_2$-pound) pork tenderloin
5 fresh ripe peaches
^{1}/$_4$ cup orange juice
^{1}/$_4$ cup white wine

Mix the olive oil with 1 teaspoon salt in a pestle or bowl. Mix the garlic with the rosemary, thyme and 1 teaspoon salt in a small bowl. Score the surface of the pork and cut a pocket lengthwise into it. Rub the pork inside and out with the olive oil mixture and then the herb mixture. Marinate, covered with waxed paper, in the refrigerator for 8 hours or longer.

Preheat the oven to 375 degrees. Dip the peaches briefly into boiling water and remove the skins. Slice the peaches. Stuff the majority of the peaches in the pocket. Insert a meat thermometer into the thickest portion of the pork. Place in a roasting pan and place the remaining peach slices around the pork. Pour the orange juice and wine around the pork.

Roast the pork, covered, for 40 minutes or to 150 degrees on the meat thermometer. Remove the pork and peaches to a platter, reserving the cooking liquid in the pan. Cook the liquid on the stovetop until reduced to a gravy consistency. Serve with the pork.

Serves 4 to 6

Simmered Spareribs with Pineapple and Bell Pepper

3 pounds pork spareribs or lean country-style ribs

1/4 cup all-purpose flour

1 to 2 teaspoons coarse salt

1/2 teaspoon freshly ground pepper

2 tablespoons vegetable oil

1 (9-ounce) can pineapple chunks or pineapple tidbits

2 tablespoons brown sugar

2 tablespoons vinegar

1/4 cup ketchup

1 small onion, cut into quarters

1 green bell pepper, cut into 1-inch squares

Shake the spareribs with the flour, salt and pepper in a paper bag, coating well. Brown the spareribs on all sides in the oil in a skillet.

Drain the pineapple, reserving the pineapple and juice. Add enough water to the juice to measure 1 1/4 cups. Combine the juice with the brown sugar, vinegar, ketchup and onion in a bowl and mix well. Pour over the ribs. Simmer, covered, for 1 1/4 hours or until tender, basting occasionally.

Stir in the bell pepper and pineapple. Simmer for 5 minutes or until the bell pepper is done to taste. Degrease the cooking liquid to serve.

Serves 6

A New Face for San Juan Capistrano

The face of the San Juan Capistrano community changed dramatically with the dissolution of the ranchos. To the multitudes of migrants coming to California, and to those seeking better lives and adventure, the area offered the promise of rich farmland and a fine climate. Farms, now smaller and diversified, produced citrus, English walnuts, barley, and other crops.

The sleepy little town of San Juan Capistrano became the center of a farming community. Residents in the area also found the commerce in San Juan and relied on the town for their needs. By the latter half of the 19th century, residents of the Capistrano Valley could enjoy shops, restaurants, hotels, and saloons.

Pork Chops with Green Apples

6 thick pork loin chops, trimmed
1 cup all-purpose flour
2 tablespoons seasoned salt
vegetable oil
6 tablespoons butter
2 or 3 tart green apples, sliced
3/4 cup packed brown sugar
1/4 teaspoon cinnamon

Shake the pork chops with the flour and seasoned salt in a bag, shaking off any excess. Fry in a small amount of oil in a skillet until brown on both sides and cooked through. Remove to a baking dish.

Preheat the oven to 300 degrees. Melt the butter in a skillet and add the apple slices. Sauté until the apples are tender-crisp. Sprinkle with the brown sugar and cinnamon and sauté until the brown sugar melts. Pour over the pork chops. Bake, covered with foil, for 20 minutes.

Note: Chopped pecans, chopped walnuts, or shredded coconut can be added to this dish for variety.

Serves 6

Sweet-and-Sour Pork

1 cup all-purpose flour

1/2 teaspoon salt

1 pound lean boneless pork, cut into 3/4-inch cubes

1 egg, beaten

vegetable oil

1/2 cup white vinegar

1/3 cup pineapple juice

1/4 cup ketchup

1 teaspoon soy sauce

1/2 cup sugar

2 tablespoons cornstarch

2 tablespoons water

1 cup drained pineapple chunks

1 small onion, thinly sliced

1 green bell pepper, cut into 1/2-inch pieces

Mix the flour and salt together. Dip the pork into the egg and then coat with the flour mixture. Heat a small amount of oil to 360 degrees in a skillet and add the pork. Stir-fry for 6 minutes or until brown on all sides. Remove to paper towels to drain.

Mix the vinegar, pineapple juice, ketchup, soy sauce and sugar in a saucepan. Bring to a boil. Blend the cornstarch with the water in a bowl. Add to the pineapple juice mixture and cook until thickened, stirring constantly. Add the pork, pineapple, onion and bell pepper. Cook for 5 minutes or until heated through. Serve with rice.

Serves 4 to 6

Barbecued Pork

3 green bell peppers, chopped
2 large onions, chopped
2 tablespoons vegetable oil
1/4 cup chili powder
3 pounds pork, cut into cubes
1 (6-ounce) can tomato paste
1/3 cup cider vinegar
2 tablespoons prepared mustard
1 tablespoon Worcestershire sauce
1 cup water
1/2 cup packed brown sugar
2 teaspoons salt
14 sandwich buns (optional)

Sauté the bell peppers and onions in the oil in a 5-quart Dutch oven over medium-high heat until tender and light brown. Stir in the chili powder and cook for 1 minute.

Add the pork, tomato paste, vinegar, prepared mustard, Worcestershire sauce, water, brown sugar and salt and mix well. Bring to a boil over high heat. Reduce the heat to low and simmer, covered, for 2 1/2 to 3 hours or until the pork is very tender and falling apart, stirring frequently and testing with a fork for doneness. Remove the pork from the cooking liquid. Shred with two forks and serve in sandwich buns.

Note: You can also degrease the liquid and return the pork to the liquid; store in the refrigerator and reheat to serve.

Serves 14

Roasted Chicken

1 (5- to 6-pound) chicken
1 lemon, cut into halves
4 garlic cloves
1/4 cup (1/2 stick) unsalted butter (optional)
olive oil

kosher salt and freshly ground pepper to taste
1 tablespoon all-purpose flour
1 cup (or more) chicken stock, water, fruit juice
 or wine

Preheat the oven to 500 degrees. Remove the wing tips from the chicken. Stuff the cavity with the lemon, garlic and butter. Drizzle with olive oil and season inside and out with kosher salt and pepper. Place breast side up in an 8×12-inch roasting pan. Place legs first in the oven and roast for 10 minutes. Move the chicken slightly in the pan to prevent sticking. Roast for 40 to 50 minutes or until the juices run clear. Remove to a platter, tilting the chicken over the roasting pan to allow all the cooking juices to drain into the pan.

Pour the cooking juices into a gravy separator, leaving any browned bits in the pan. Allow the juices to separate and spoon 1 tablespoon of the drippings from the top into the roasting pan. Place on the stovetop and stir the flour into the drippings. Cook over medium heat until slightly brown, stirring constantly.

Pour the juice from the bottom of the gravy separator into a 2-cup measure, taking care not to get any of the grease. Add enough stock to measure 1½ cups. Add to the roasting pan and cook for 4 minutes or until thickened, stirring constantly. Serve with the chicken.

Serves 2 to 4

Chicken Fajitas

2 tablespoons vegetable oil

1 pound boneless skinless chicken breasts,
  cut into 1/2× 1-inch strips

2 1/2 teaspoons Fajita Seasoning Mix (below)

1/4 teaspoon salt

1 large green bell pepper, cut into strips

1 large red bell pepper, cut into strips

1 onion, cut into strips

1 tablespoon chopped cilantro

flour tortillas, warmed

sour cream and salsa to taste

Heat the oil in a 12-inch skillet over medium heat. Add the chicken, Fajita Seasoning and salt and sauté for 5 to 6 minutes or until the chicken is no longer pink, stirring occasionally. Add the green bell pepper, red bell pepper and onion and sauté for 5 to 6 minutes longer or until the chicken is cooked through and the peppers are tender-crisp. Stir in the cilantro. Serve in warm tortillas and top with sour cream and salsa if desired.

Serves 4

Fajita Seasoning Mix

1 tablespoon chili powder

1 tablespoon garlic powder

1 1/2 teaspoons paprika

1 1/2 teaspoons salt

1 tablespoon white pepper

1 1/2 teaspoons black pepper

Mix the chili powder, garlic powder, paprika, salt, white pepper and black pepper in an airtight jar. Use as seasoning for fajitas.

Makes 1/4 cup

Chicken Marsala

1 cup all-purpose flour

1 teaspoon salt

1 teaspoon pepper

4 (5- to 6-ounce) boneless skinless chicken breasts, trimmed

2 tablespoons olive oil

1/4 cup (1/2 stick) butter

8 ounces white mushrooms, sliced

2 1/2 ounces pancetta, chopped

1 garlic clove, crushed

1 tablespoon tomato paste

1 1/2 cups sweet marsala

1 1/2 teaspoons fresh lemon juice

2 tablespoons minced fresh parsley

Preheat the oven to 350 degrees. Mix the flour, salt and pepper together and add the chicken, turning to coat well. Brown the chicken in a mixture of the olive oil and butter in a skillet. Remove to an 8×8-inch baking dish.

Sauté the mushrooms in the olive oil in the skillet. Add to the chicken. Add the pancetta and garlic to the skillet and sauté for several minutes. Stir in the tomato paste, wine, lemon juice and parsley. Pour over the chicken. Bake for 45 minutes or until the chicken is cooked through and tender.

Serves 4

Chicken Parmesan

4 boneless skinless chicken breasts

2 (14-ounce) cans stewed Italian-style tomatoes

2 tablespoons cornstarch

1/2 teaspoon oregano

1/4 cup (1 ounce) grated Parmesan cheese

Preheat the oven to 425 degrees. Spray an 8×8-inch baking pan with nonstick cooking spray and arrange the chicken in the prepared pan. Bake for 15 to 20 minutes or until the chicken is cooked through.

Combine the tomatoes, cornstarch and oregano in a saucepan and mix well. Cook over medium heat until thickened, stirring constantly. Spread over the chicken and sprinkle with the cheese. Bake for 5 minutes or until the cheese melts.

Note: You can add a few drops of hot red pepper sauce or a sprinkle of garlic to the sauce to increase the flavor or top with sliced mozzarella cheese during the last 5 minutes of the baking time.

Serves 4

Bougainvillea in bloom at the Mission

Artichoke Chicken Capistrano

2 (6-ounce) jars marinated artichoke hearts

3 tablespoons extra-virgin olive oil

8 boneless skinless chicken breasts

1/4 cup all-purpose flour

1 (28-ounce) can diced Italian-style tomatoes

1 pound sliced cremini or white mushrooms

3 garlic cloves, minced

1/4 cup chopped fresh basil

1 teaspoon dried oregano, or 1 tablespoon chopped fresh oregano

1 cup dry white wine

3 tablespoons minced fresh Italian parsley

Preheat the oven to 350 degrees. Drain the artichokes, reserving the artichokes and the marinade. Combine half the reserved marinade with the olive oil in a large skillet and heat over medium-high heat. Coat the chicken with the flour and add to the skillet. Cook until brown on both sides. Remove to a baking dish.

Add the tomatoes, mushrooms, garlic, basil, oregano and wine to the skillet, stirring up any browned bits. Simmer over medium-low heat for 10 to 15 minutes or until heated through. Pour over the chicken.

Bake for 30 minutes. Adjust the seasonings to taste and stir in the reserved artichokes. Bake for 10 minutes longer. Sprinkle with the parsley and serve with spaghetti or fettuccine.

Note: Take care not to overcook the chicken. Because boneless chicken breasts vary in size, test them for doneness and adjust the baking time accordingly.

Serves 6 to 8

Father Greg's Chicken with Pasta

Since Father Greg Marquez, parochial vicar of Mission San Juan Capistrano from 2003 to 2007, cooks rarely. His recipes show that he usually makes creative leftovers. When there is leftover roasted chicken, he shreds it, discarding the skin and bones. He cooks linguini for nine minutes or until al dente, drains it, and returns it to the saucepan. He adds the shredded chicken, one container of prepared pesto and mixes well, taking care not to break up the pasta. He serves it with Parmesan cheese and a little pepper.

Lemon Chicken Pasta

1 teaspoon olive oil
2 garlic cloves, minced
6 ounces boneless skinless
   chicken breasts, cut into
   1/2-inch strips
1/2 cup frozen peas, thawed
1/3 cup coarsely shredded carrots
1/2 cup low-sodium chicken broth
2 tablespoons light cream cheese

2 cups cooked farfalle
3 tablespoons grated
   Parmesan cheese
2 teaspoons lemon juice
1 teaspoon rosemary or
   Italian seasoning
1/2 teaspoon salt
1/8 teaspoon pepper
chopped fresh chives (optional)

Spray a large nonstick skillet with nonstick cooking spray and pour in the olive oil. Heat over medium-high heat and add the garlic. Sauté for 15 seconds. Add the chicken and sauté for 1 minute. Add the peas and carrots and sauté for 1 minute. Remove the chicken and vegetables to a bowl with a slotted spoon.

Combine the broth and cream cheese in the skillet. Cook over medium heat for 3 minutes or until the cream cheese melts, whisking to mix well. Add the chicken mixture, pasta, Parmesan cheese, lemon juice, rosemary, salt and pepper and mix well. Cook for 1 minute or until heated through. Sprinkle with chopped fresh chives.

Serves 2

Chicken Sauté with Prosciutto and Mushrooms

2 pounds boneless chicken breasts and/or thighs

coarse salt and freshly ground pepper to taste

all-purpose flour

vegetable oil

1/3 cup finely chopped onion

1/4 cup chopped shallots

2 garlic cloves, finely minced

1/4 cup (1/2 stick) butter

4 ounces prosciutto, finely juilienned

2 teaspoons dried tarragon, or

    1 tablespoon chopped fresh tarragon

3/4 cup dried porcini mushrooms

3 tablespoons lemon juice

3/4 cup dry white wine

1/4 cup (1/2 stick) butter

Cut the chicken into small serving pieces. Sprinkle with salt and pepper and coat lightly with flour. Pour oil to a depth of 1/3 inch in a large heavy skillet and add the chicken in batches, frying until golden brown on all sides. Remove the chicken and drain.

Sauté the onion, shallots and garlic in 1/4 cup butter in the skillet until tender. Add the prosciutto and sauté lightly. Sprinkle with the tarragon and cook for 3 minutes. Return the chicken to the skillet.

Combine the mushrooms with just enough water to cover in a saucepan. Bring to a boil and reduce the heat. Simmer for 1 minute; drain, reserving the cooking liquid. Add the mushrooms, lemon juice and wine to the skillet. Stir in enough of the reserved mushroom cooking liquid to reach the desired consistency.

Simmer for 5 minutes. Stir in 1/4 cup butter and cook until the butter melts, stirring to mix well. Serve with risotto or linguini.

Serves 6 to 8

Mexican Chicken Pasta Casserole

2 tablespoons butter

2 teaspoons salad herbs

$1/3$ cup grated Parmesan cheese

2 cups cooked egg noodles

1 tablespoon chopped onion

1 garlic clove, minced

2 teaspoons olive oil

1 large tomato, chopped

4 green chiles, sliced and cooked

$1/8$ teaspoon paprika

$1/8$ teaspoon thyme

$1/2$ teaspoon salt

$1/4$ teaspoon coarsely ground pepper

$1/2$ cup chicken stock or chicken broth

$1^1/2$ cups cooked chicken strips

2 tablespoons finely chopped pimento

2 cups (8 ounces) shredded Cheddar cheese

Preheat the oven to 350 degrees. Add the butter, salad herbs and Parmesan cheese to the noodles in a bowl and mix well. Cover and set aside.

Sauté the onion and garlic in the olive oil in a saucepan. Add the tomato, green chiles, paprika, thyme, salt and pepper. Stir in the stock and chicken strips. Simmer for 10 to 15 minutes or until heated through, stirring occasionally.

Combine the noodles, pimento and $1^1/2$ cups of the Cheddar cheese with the chicken mixture in the saucepan and mix gently. Spoon into a baking dish and top with the remaining $1/2$ cup Cheddar cheese. Bake for 10 to 15 minutes or until the cheese melts.

Serves 4 to 6

Chicken Tortilla Casserole

Cheese Sauce

1/4 cup (1/2 stick) butter

1/3 cup all-purpose flour

3 cups milk

8 ounces sharp Cheddar cheese, shredded

salt and pepper to taste

Casserole

1/4 cup chopped onion

2 teaspoons butter or olive oil

1 pound chicken, cooked, cooled and
   cut into cubes

8 ounces Monterey Jack cheese, shredded
   or cubed

4 ounces mild green chile salsa

3/4 cup sour cream or light sour cream

8 to 10 medium flour tortillas

For the sauce, melt the butter in a medium saucepan over medium-low heat. Stir in the flour and cook for 2 to 3 minutes or until bubbly. Remove from the heat and stir in the milk gradually. Cook over medium heat until thickened and heated through, stirring constantly. Add the cheese and cook until the cheese melts, stirring constantly. Season with salt and pepper.

For the casserole, preheat the oven to 350 degrees. Spray a 9×13-inch or larger baking pan with nonstick cooking spray. Sauté the onion in the butter in a small sauté pan. Combine the chicken, cheese, salsa, sautéed onion and sour cream in a bowl and mix well. Place about 1/2 cup of the chicken mixture on each tortilla and roll the tortillas to enclose the filling. Arrange seam side down in the prepared pan; use another pan if necessary to avoid crowding the rolls.

Pour the sauce over the tortilla rolls and bake for 45 minutes. Serve immediately. You can also prepare the casserole 24 hours in advance and chill, covered, in the refrigerator. This will allow the rolls to absorb the sauce and they will puff when baked. Let come to room temperature before baking.

Note: Use leftover chicken or cook chicken in the microwave for this recipe. Combine the chicken with a small amount of water or chicken broth, salt, and pepper in a microwave-safe dish. Microwave, covered, on High for 3 minutes or longer; do not overcook.

Serves 6 to 8

Mexicale Turkey, Chicken, or Steak

Combine 1 thinly sliced onion,
2 minced garlic cloves, the juice of
2 lemons and 1/4 cup packed brown
sugar in a bowl. Add 1 tablespoon
Mexican oregano, 1 teaspoon
thyme, 2 tablespoons chili powder,
1 tablespoon paprika and
2 teaspoons salt and mix well. Add
2 pounds thinly sliced turkey breast,
chicken breasts, or beef to the
mixture and marinate in the
refrigerator for 1 hour or longer.
Remove from the marinade and grill
over hot coals. Cut into thin strips
and serve on warm tortillas with
chopped tomatoes, chopped onions,
chopped cilantro, salsa fresca,
Mexican cream and/or guacamole.

Party Chicken Casserole

8 ounces Monterey Jack cheese
6 boneless skinless chicken breasts
6 slices dried beef
3 thick slices lean bacon, cut crosswise into halves
3/4 cup sour cream
1 (10-ounce) can cream of mushroom soup
1/4 cup tomato paste
1/2 cup chopped red bell pepper or chopped pimento
chopped parsley to taste

Preheat the oven to 350 degrees. Shred 2 ounces of the cheese and cut the remaining cheese into six 2-inch sticks. Pound the chicken slightly. Place one slice of dried beef on each chicken breast and top with one cheese stick. Roll the chicken to enclose the beef and cheese and place seam side down in a greased baking dish. Top each roll with half a bacon slice.

Combine the sour cream, soup, shredded cheese and tomato paste in a bowl and mix well. Spread evenly over the chicken rolls and sprinkle with the chopped red bell pepper and parsley. Bake for 1 to 1 1/4 hours.

Note: You may prepare this dish in advance, double wrap in foil and freeze until needed. Bring to room temperature before baking.

Serves 6 to 8

Florentine Fish

6 fillets of salmon, trout, sole, turbot or halibut (about 2 to 2$^{1}/_{2}$ pounds)

1$^{1}/_{2}$ cups dry white wine

2 egg yolks

1 cup cream or heavy cream

1 tablespoon all-purpose flour

1 tablespoon butter, softened

$^{1}/_{4}$ teaspoon basil

$^{1}/_{4}$ teaspoon dill weed

$^{2}/_{3}$ cup freshly grated Parmesan cheese

2 tablespoons lemon juice

$^{1}/_{8}$ teaspoon nutmeg

salt and pepper to taste

2$^{1}/_{2}$ cups chopped fresh spinach, or 2 (10-ounce) packages frozen chopped spinach

Preheat the oven to 350 degrees. Combine the fish with the wine in a heavy shallow saucepan. Poach over low heat for 6 to 10 minutes or until cooked through. Remove the fish to a plate and reserve the poaching liquid in the saucepan. Blend the egg yolks and cream in a small bowl. Add to the poaching liquid gradually and cook until smooth, stirring constantly.

Blend the flour with the butter in a small bowl. Add to the poaching liquid with the basil and dill weed. Cook over low heat until thickened, stirring constantly. Reserve 2 to 3 tablespoons of the cheese and stir the remaining cheese into the liquid with the lemon juice and nutmeg; season with salt and pepper.

Cook the spinach in a small amount of water in a 1$^{1}/_{2}$- to 2-quart saucepan. Drain and squeeze to remove as much liquid as possible. Spread in a greased shallow 2-quart baking dish and spread with half the wine mixture. Layer the fish in the prepared dish and top with the remaining wine mixture. Sprinkle with the reserved cheese.

Bake for 20 to 30 minutes or until bubbly. Finish by broiling for 1 to 2 minutes or until light brown. Serve with fresh French bread and a crisp green salad.

Serves 6

Grilled Halibut with Balsamic Vinegar

1 (16-ounce) bottle balsamic vinaigrette
1/2 bottle dry white wine
4 halibut steaks

1/2 (3-ounce) bottle capers
1 (4-ounce) can sliced black olives
1 tomato, chopped (optional)

Mix the balsamic vinaigrette and white wine in a large shallow nonreactive pan that can be placed on the grill. Add the fish steaks to the marinade; the level of the marinade should reach halfway up the fish. Marinate in the refrigerator for 2 hours or longer, turning once.

Preheat the grill. Place the pan with the fish and marinade on the grill. Remove the fish to the grill rack, leaving the pan with the marinade on the grill. Grill the fish until brown on both sides. Return the fish to the marinade and sprinkle with the capers, black olives and tomato. Cook on the grill for 10 minutes longer. Remove the fish to a serving platter. Pour the hot marinade into a bowl to serve with the fish.

Serves 4

Baked Salmon in Parchment

1 (4- to 6-ounce) salmon steak per person
salt and pepper to taste
1/2 small Roma tomato per person,
     seeded and chopped
1/4 to 1/2 garlic clove per person, crushed

2 tablespoons chopped kalamata olives per person
1 thin slice lemon per person
1 teaspoon capers per person
1 teaspoon extra-virgin olive oil per person
1 sprig of fresh dill weed per person

Preheat the oven to 350 degrees. Place each salmon steak in the center of a large square of parchment paper. Season with salt and pepper. Place the tomato, garlic, olives, lemon, capers, olive oil and dill weed on top of the salmon. Fold the parchment paper to enclose the salmon and place on a baking sheet. Bake for 20 to 30 minutes or until the salmon flakes easily. Unwrap the packages and slide the salmon onto a serving plate.

Makes a variable amount

Pesto-Stuffed Salmon

Pesto

$1/2$ cup packed chopped fresh basil

$1/4$ cup packed chopped fresh parsley

$1/2$ cup (2 ounces) grated Parmesan cheese

1 garlic clove

1 tablespoon (or more) olive oil

kosher salt and freshly ground pepper to taste

Salmon

4 (6- to 8-ounce) salmon fillets

lemon juice

olive oil

salt and pepper to taste

For the pesto, combine the basil, parsley, cheese and garlic in a blender. Add the olive oil and season with kosher salt and pepper. Process until smooth, adding additional olive oil if needed for the desired consistency.

For the salmon, preheat the oven to 350 degrees. Line a baking pan with baking parchment or foil and grease the parchment or foil. Cut a pocket in each salmon fillet and stuff evenly with the pesto mixture. Arrange in the prepared baking pan and drizzle with lemon juice and olive oil; season lightly with salt and pepper. Bake for 20 minutes or until cooked through.

Serves 4

Poached Salmon

Poached Salmon Sauce

1/4 cup cider vinegar

1/2 cup vegetable oil

1/2 cup chili sauce

2 teaspoons Worcestershire sauce

2 tablespoons sugar

1 teaspoon dry mustard

1 teaspoon salt

Salmon

1 large onion

1 rib celery

2 carrots, peeled

1/2 cup cider vinegar

1 bay leaf

1 cup white wine

1 (5- to 7-pound) whole or half salmon

For the sauce, combine the vinegar, oil, chili sauce and Worcestershire sauce in a bowl and mix well. Stir in the sugar, dry mustard and salt.

For the salmon, combine the onion, celery, carrots, vinegar and bay leaf in a saucepan. Bring to a simmer and add the wine. Add enough water to cover the vegetables. Cook until the vegetables are tender. Place the salmon on the vegetables; add additional water if needed to cover the salmon. Simmer, covered, for 20 to 30 minutes or until the salmon is tender.

Let the salmon stand in the stock until cool. Remove the salmon from the cooking liquid, discarding the liquid and vegetables. Spoon some of the sauce over the salmon and garnish with thin lemon slices and chopped parsley. Pour the remaining sauce into a sauceboat or pitcher to serve.

Note: Do not use steaks or fillets for this recipe.

Serves 4 to 6

The Bells are Ringing
A CALL TO TABLE

Red Snapper with Tomato and Caper Sauce

1 large yellow onion, finely chopped

3 garlic cloves, minced

3 tablespoons olive oil

1 (28-ounce) can peeled tomatoes, chopped

1/4 cup dry white wine

2 tablespoons chopped parsley

2 tablespoons capers

1 teaspoon crushed oregano

1/2 teaspoon salt

1/4 teaspoon pepper

1 1/2 pounds skinless red snapper, salmon or other white fish

Preheat the oven to 450 degrees. Sauté the onion and garlic in the olive oil until tender but not brown. Stir in the tomatoes, wine, parsley, capers, oregano, salt and pepper. Bring to a boil and reduce the heat. Simmer for 10 to 15 minutes or until the desired consistency.

Place the fish in a baking dish and pour the sauce over the top. Bake for 12 to 20 minutes or until the fish flakes easily. Remove the fish to a serving platter and spoon the sauce over the top. Garnish with additional chopped parsley.

Serves 4 to 6

*Father
St. John O'Sullivan,
the Great Restorer,
1874-1933*

*Father St. John O'Sullivan was a man
of passionate vision and dedication.
When he arrived at Mission
San Juan Capistrano in 1910,
he was sick and considered too frail
for active work in the divine service.
The doctors had given up hope
for his recovery, but the Mission
gave him the strength and
inspiration to keep moving forward
for another twenty-three years.
The place reminded him of himself,
suffering from decay and near death.
He patiently began restoration
efforts of historic proportions over
the next two decades,*

continued ➤

The Bells are Ringing
A CALL TO TABLE

Sea Bass with Roasted Tomatoes

Roasted Tomatoes

4 Roma tomatoes
olive oil
crushed garlic
chopped fresh thyme
sea salt

Sea Bass

4 sea bass fillets
4 thin slices prosciutto
olive oil
chopped fresh thyme

For the tomatoes, preheat the oven to 350 degrees. Cut the tomatoes into halves lengthwise and arrange skin side down in a single layer in a lightly oiled baking pan. Drizzle with olive oil and sprinkle with garlic, thyme and sea salt. Roast for 30 to 40 minutes or until done to taste. Maintain the oven temperature.

For the sea bass, wrap each fillet with a slice of prosciutto. Arrange in a single layer in a baking pan. Drizzle with olive oil and sprinkle with thyme. Bake for 15 to 20 minutes or until the fish flakes easily. Place two roasted tomato halves on each fillet to serve. Serve with rice or risotto.

Note: If you place the fish in the oven about 20 minutes after the tomatoes, the tomatoes and fish will be done at about the same time.

Serves 4

Tuna Steaks with Tarragon Butter

Tarragon Butter

- 1/4 teaspoon lemon juice
- 1/2 teaspoon chopped fresh tarragon, or 1/4 teaspoon dried tarragon
- 2 tablespoons butter, softened

Tuna

- 2 (8-ounce) tuna steaks, 3/4 inch thick
- 1/4 teaspoon salt
- 1/4 teaspoon pepper
- 1 tablespoon olive oil

For the butter, combine the lemon juice and tarragon with the butter in a small bowl and mix until smooth. Shape into a log 1 inch long. Cover and chill until firm.

For the tuna, sprinkle the steaks with salt and pepper. Brown in the olive oil in a skillet for 5 minutes on each side or until done to taste; do not overcook. Slice the butter and serve on the steaks.

Serves 2

Artists at work in the Mission Gardens

including clearing away the weeds and rubble, building shelter for himself, and reinforcing the adobe brick structures. To everyone's surprise, including his own, he did not die but worked vigorously for twenty years toward the impossible dream of renewing the ruins of Mission San Juan Capistrano. Serving as pastor of the Mission from 1910 until his death in 1933, he inspired the local population to see the restoration of the Mission as a legacy for future generations. He opened the grounds to landscape painters and photographers whose romantic depictions of the Mission ruins attracted even more supporters for the restoration effort. Father O'Sullivan is buried in the Mission cemetery located immediately east of the Serra Chapel.

The Bells are Ringing
A CALL TO TABLE

Stuffed Sole

4 ounces mushrooms, sliced	3 pounds sole fillets
1/2 cup finely chopped white onion	salt and pepper to taste
2 tablespoons chopped parsley	2 (10-ounce) cans cream of mushroom soup
2 tablespoons butter	1/3 cup white wine
4 1/2 ounces fresh or canned shrimp, chopped	1/2 cup (2 ounces) shredded Cheddar cheese

Preheat the oven to 375 degrees. Sauté the mushrooms, onion and parsley in the butter in a skillet until light golden brown. Stir in the shrimp. Arrange the sole fillets on a work surface and sprinkle with salt and pepper. Spoon the shrimp filling onto the fillets and roll to enclose the filling. Arrange seam side down in a greased baking pan. Mix the soup and wine in a bowl. Spoon over the rolls. Bake for 35 to 40 minutes or until the fish flakes easily. Sprinkle with the cheese and bake just until light brown.

Serves 4

Sole with Lemon Cream

2 tablespoons unsalted butter	3/4 cup cream or heavy cream
2 pounds sole fillets, cut to make 4 pieces	grated zest of 1 lemon
1/2 teaspoon salt	1/4 teaspoon salt
1/4 teaspoon freshly ground pepper	1 tablespoon lemon juice
1/4 cup all-purpose flour	2 tablespoons chopped fresh parsley

Melt the butter in a skillet over medium heat. Sprinkle the sole fillets with 1/2 teaspoon salt and the pepper. Dredge the fillets in the flour and shake to remove any excess. Sauté the fillets in the butter for 2 minutes per side or until the fish flakes easily; do not overcook. Remove to a serving dish and keep warm.

Add the cream and lemon zest to the skillet. Simmer for 2 minutes or until the cream begins to thicken, stirring constantly. Stir in 1/4 teaspoon salt, the lemon juice and parsley. Spoon over the fillets.

Serves 4

Scallops with Orange Sauce

Orange Sauce

juice and grated zest of 2 oranges

1 shallot, chopped

1/2 cup (1 stick) butter

Scallops

8 to 12 slices bacon

8 to 12 scallops

For the sauce, combine the orange juice, orange zest and shallot in a small saucepan. Cook until the liquid is reduced to a thick consistency. Combine with the butter in a food processor and process until creamy. Store in the refrigerator if not using immediately and reheat before serving.

For the scallops, preheat the oven to 375 degrees. Cook the bacon in a skillet until partially cooked but not crisp. Wrap one slice of bacon around each scallop and secure with a wooden pick. Arrange in a baking pan. Bake for 10 to 20 minutes or until the scallops are cooked through and the bacon is crisp. Place the scallops on a plate and pour the sauce around them.

Serves 4

Curried Shrimp

1/4 cup (1/2 stick) butter, melted

1/4 cup all-purpose flour

1 1/2 cups milk

1/4 cup sherry

1/4 cup ketchup

1/2 teaspoon salt

1/4 teaspoon sweet paprika

2 teaspoons curry powder, or to taste

8 ounces shrimp, shelled and deveined

2 cups cooked rice

Melt the butter in a saucepan. Add the flour and cook until bubbly. Remove from the heat and slowly stir in the milk. Cook over medium heat until thickened, stirring constantly. Add the wine, ketchup, salt, paprika and curry powder. Reduce the heat to low and simmer for 3 minutes. Add the shrimp and cook until the shrimp are pink. Do not overcook. Spoon over the rice. Serve topped with chopped peanuts or other nuts, chopped green onions, chutney, shredded coconut or chopped cooked bacon, if desired.

Serves 2 to 4

Garlic Shrimp

1/2 cup (1 stick) butter

1/2 onion, chopped

1 bunch green onions, chopped

1 tablespoon chopped garlic

1/2 green bell pepper, chopped

1 (8-ounce) can water chestnuts, chopped

1 (8-ounce) can pineapple tidbits or crushed pineapple

crystallized ginger to taste

2 tablespoons jalapeño jelly

31 to 40 extra-large shrimp, peeled and deveined with the tails intact

2 tablespoons lemon juice or lime juice

2 tablespoons soy sauce

2 tablespoons sesame seeds

1/4 teaspoon pepper

2 teaspoons cornstarch

1 cup warm water

Melt the butter in a skillet over medium heat. Add the onion, green onions, garlic, bell pepper, water chestnuts, pineapple, ginger and jalapeño jelly. Sauté for 4 to 5 minutes or until the onion is tender-crisp. Add the shrimp, lemon juice, soy sauce, sesame seeds and pepper. Sauté for several minutes.

Blend the cornstarch with the water in a bowl. Add to the skillet and cook until the mixture thickens and the shrimp are cooked through, stirring constantly; do not overcook, as the shrimp will become tough.

Note: Spice Hunter brand of crystallized ginger was used for testing purposes in this recipe. The shrimp can also be served as an appetizer.

Serves 4 to 6

Shrimp Piccata

1/2 cup dry white wine

1/2 cup chicken broth

2 tablespoons lemon juice

1/4 teaspoon salt

freshly ground pepper to taste

1 pound fresh or frozen medium to large shrimp, peeled and deveined

2 tablespoons all-purpose flour

1 tablespoon (or more) butter or margarine

1 tablespoon (or more) olive oil

2 green onions, minced with some of the green portion

1 garlic clove, minced

2 tablespoons drained capers

hot cooked brown rice and white rice

Mix the wine, broth, lemon juice, salt and pepper in a bowl. Toss the shrimp with the flour in a bowl, coating well.

Melt the butter with the olive oil in a heated wok or skillet. Add the shrimp half at a time and stir-fry for 2 to 3 minutes or until opaque, adding additional butter or olive oil if needed. Remove the shrimp to a bowl. Add the green onions and garlic to the wok and stir-fry lightly. Stir the wine mixture and add to the wok. Cook until bubbly and the liquid is slightly reduced, stirring constantly. Return the shrimp to the wok and add the capers. Cook for 1 minute or until heated through. Serve immediately over a mixture of brown and white rice. Garnish with lemon slices.

Serves 6

Dana Point Seafood Feast

Tomato Sauce

1^1/$_2$ cups finely chopped seeded tomatoes

1 bunch green onions, finely chopped
   (about 6 green onions)

2 tablespoons julienned fresh basil

1 tablespoon butter

^{1}/$_2$ cup white wine

juice of 1 lemon

salt and pepper to taste

Seafood

4 teaspoons minced garlic

^{1}/$_2$ cup virgin olive oil

1 tablespoon butter

1 cup white wine

12 fresh clams

12 fresh mussels

12 cooked prawns

For the sauce, sauté the tomatoes, green onions and basil in the butter in a saucepan. Add the wine and lemon juice and season with salt and pepper. Simmer for 15 to 20 minutes.

For the seafood, sauté the garlic in the olive and butter in a large saucepan until the garlic is cooked through but not brown. Add the wine, clams and mussels. Bring to a boil and cook until the shells open; discard any clams or mussels that do not open. Add the prawns.

Remove the seafood with a slotted spoon from the broth to a bowl. Add the hot tomato sauce and mix well. Serve immediately with crusty French bread.

Serves 4

Baked Broccoli

1 1/4 pounds fresh broccoli, trimmed

2 eggs, lightly beaten

1 cup cream of mushroom soup

1/2 cup (2 ounces) shredded Cheddar cheese

2 tablespoons chopped green onions

1 teaspoon hot red pepper sauce

pepper to taste

1 1/2 cups soft white bread crumbs

2 tablespoons butter, melted

Preheat the oven to 350 degrees. Cut the broccoli into serving-size pieces. Steam, covered, until tender-crisp; drain.

Combine the eggs, soup, cheese, green onions, hot sauce, pepper and half the bread crumbs in a bowl and mix well. Fold in the broccoli. Spoon into a 1 1/2-quart baking dish. Combine the remaining bread crumbs with the butter in a bowl. Sprinkle over the broccoli. Bake for 35 minutes.

Serves 6 to 8

Sweet-and-Sour Red Cabbage

1 cup (2 sticks) butter

2 tablespoons cider vinegar

2 tablespoons water

2 tablespoons sugar

1/2 teaspoon salt

1 (2 1/2-pound) head red cabbage, shredded

1 cup red currant jelly

ground cloves to taste

Melt the butter in a 6-quart saucepan and stir in the vinegar, water, sugar and salt. Add the cabbage and cook, covered, over low heat for 1 hour or until the cabbage is tender. Stir in the jelly and cloves just before serving. Serve hot with pork roast or pork chops.

Serves 4 to 6

Carrots Glazed with Ginger and Honey

6 cups water

3/4 teaspoon salt

3 pounds small young carrots with tops, peeled,
  or 1 (3-pound) package peeled baby carrots

2 tablespoons butter

2 tablespoons honey

4 teaspoons minced fresh ginger

Bring the water and salt to a boil in a heavy 12- to 14-inch skillet. Trim carrot tops to 2 inches. Add the carrots to the skillet and return to a boil. Reduce the heat and simmer, covered, for 10 to 12 minutes or just until the carrots are tender; drain. Remove carefully to a baking sheet lined with paper towels, taking care to preserve the green carrot tops. Pat dry with additional paper towels.

Combine the butter, honey and ginger in the same skillet. Cook over medium heat until the butter melts, stirring constantly. Add the carrots carefully and cook for 2 to 3 minutes or until the carrots are glazed, stirring gently. Arrange the carrots in a shallow dish or on a platter and drizzle with the remaining glaze.

Note: The carrots may be cooked a day in advance. Cool and chill, covered, in the refrigerator. Let stand at room temperature for 1 hour before glazing. Heat in the glaze for 4 to 5 minutes.

Serves 10 to 12

Creamed Corn Casserole

1 (14-ounce) cream-style corn
2 tablespoons flour
2 tablespoons sugar
2 eggs, beaten
1 tablespoon grated Parmesan cheese

Preheat the oven to 350 degrees. Combine the corn, flour, sugar, eggs and cheese in a bowl and mix well. Pour into a 1-quart baking dish sprayed with nonstick cooking spray. Bake for 40 to 45 minutes or until set. Do not overbake.

Serves 4

Balsamic-Braised Onions

3 (10-ounce) packages fresh
   white pearl onions, trimmed
1 1/2 cups water
2 tablespoons unsalted butter

2 tablespoons honey
1 teaspoon coarse salt
2 tablespoons balsamic vinegar

Bring enough water to cover the onions to a boil in a saucepan. Prepare an ice water bath. Add the onions to the boiling water and cook for 3 minutes. Drain the onions and plunge into the ice water bath.

Peel the onions and combine with 1 1/2 cups water, the butter, honey and salt in a large nonstick skillet. Cook over medium-high heat for 30 minutes or until the water evaporates and the onions begin to brown. Reduce the heat to medium and stir in the vinegar. Cook for 15 minutes longer or until the onions are caramelized, stirring frequently to avoid burning.

Serves 4 to 6

Black Beans

Bring 4 cups black beans with water to cover to a boil in a large saucepan. Turn off the heat and let stand for 1 hour. Add 3 mild chiles and 1 jalapeño chile that have been roasted, seeded, and chopped. Add 2 chopped onions, 1 tablespoon minced garlic, 2 cups chopped seeded tomatoes, 1 tablespoon dried oregano, 2 teaspoons cumin, 1/2 teaspoon cayenne pepper and 1 teaspoon salt. Cook for 2 to 2 1/2 hours or until the beans are tender. Garnish servings with chopped cilantro.

Jacque Nuñez

Jacque Nuñez is the Mission San Juan Capistrano's Juañeno/Acjachemen storyteller. In her California Indian presentation, she speaks of her ancestors' foods: wi'wish (acorn mush), rabbit, seeds, berries, abalone, deer, even roasted grasshoppers! She is a descendent of the Leather Jacket soldier, Feliciano Rios, who guarded Father Serra. Most Juañeros, along with their cuisine, are the blend of two cultures.

continued ➤

Calabacitas de la Familia Rios (Rios Family Zucchini)

1/4 cup vegetable oil

6 zucchini, or 2 each green zucchini, yellow zucchini and yellow crookneck squash, coarsely chopped

1/2 yellow onion, chopped

2 green onions, sliced

2 fresh Anaheim chiles, sliced

3 garlic cloves, minced

1 (16-ounce) can whole tomatoes

1 (16-ounce) can whole kernel corn, drained

garlic salt, salt and pepper to taste

1/2 cup (2 ounces) shredded Monterey Jack cheese

Heat the oil in a large skillet over high heat and add the zucchini. Stir-fry for 1 to 2 minutes. Add the yellow onion, green onions, chiles and garlic. Stir-fry for 3 to 5 minutes or until the vegetables are light brown.

Add the tomatoes, corn, garlic salt, salt and pepper. Bring to a boil and reduce the heat. Simmer, covered, for 15 to 20 minutes or until the desired consistency. Sprinkle with the cheese just before serving.

Serves 8

Jacque Nuñez, Juañeno/Acjachemen descendent and performer with students visiting the Mission

Oven-Roasted Vegetables

4 white, red or new potatoes
    potatoes, cut into quarters
12 small carrots, peeled
12 small boiling onions
2 tablespoons extra-virgin olive oil
2 garlic cloves, minced or crushed
1 teaspoon herbes de Provence
1 teaspoon seasoned salt

$1/2$ teaspoon freshly ground pepper
1 teaspoon finely chopped fresh
    rosemary, or $1/2$ teaspoon
    dried rosemary
4 to 6 small Roma tomatoes,
    cut into halves and seeded
extra-virgin olive oil, salt and
    freshly ground pepper to taste

Place the potatoes, carrots and onions in a large sealable plastic bag. Combine 2 tablespoons olive oil with the garlic, herbes de Provence, seasoned salt, $1/2$ teaspoon pepper and rosemary in a bowl and mix well. Pour over the vegetables, seal the bag and mix gently. Marinate in the refrigerator for up to 2 hours.

Preheat the oven to 425 degrees. Remove the vegetables to two large baking sheets lined with foil; do not crowd to ensure even browning. Roast for 5 minutes.

Arrange the tomatoes on a baking sheet. Drizzle with additional olive oil and season with salt and pepper to taste. Place in the oven. Roast the potato mixture and the tomatoes together for 15 minutes longer or until evenly brown. Remove to a heated platter and serve with roasted meat or fowl.

Serves 8

Although Jacque loves the favorite recipes—treats such as abondigos soup, chili verde, and frijoles de jolla—that she has learned by watching her mother and aunts cook at their restaurant, Casa de Los Rios, she has chosen to share the calabacitas recipe written about in the Register because of its more precise instructions. Her other favorite family gift is the expression "Mi casa es su casa," or "My home is your home." She loves nothing more than to share her evening meal with a friend, no phone call necessary!

Mexican Rice

This Mexican or Spanish dish would
have been baked in the horno along
with meat and beans as the horno
was cooling down. Today, it can be
prepared in the oven. Sauté 4 ounces
ground or finely chopped salt pork in
a heavy ovenproof pot until light
brown. Add 1/2 cup finely chopped
onion, 1/2 cup finely chopped
green or red bell pepper, and
1 minced garlic clove and sauté until
tender. Add 1 cup long grain rice and
sauté for 5 minutes. Add 11/2 cups
chicken stock or vegetable stock,
1 cup chopped canned tomatoes,
1/2 teaspoon hot or sweet paprika
and 1/4 teaspoon ground pepper.
Bring to a boil. Bake at 350 degrees
for about 25 minutes or
until the rice is tender.

continued ➤

The Bells are Ringing
A CALL TO TABLE

Orzo Baked with Greek Cheeses

1 (14-ounce) can chicken broth
salt to taste
16 ounces orzo
1/2 cup cream or heavy cream
1/4 cup olive oil
8 ounces feta cheese, crumbled
1 tablespoon chopped fresh dill weed
pepper to taste
1/3 cup grated Kasseri cheese or Romano cheese

Preheat the oven to 350 degrees. Pour the broth into a 4-quart saucepan and
add enough water to nearly fill the saucepan. Add salt to taste and bring to a boil.
Stir in the orzo and cook al dente or just until tender but slightly firm to the bite,
stirring occasionally. Drain and return to the saucepan.

Add the cream, olive oil, feta cheese and dill weed to the orzo and season with
salt and pepper. Spoon into a 11/2-quart baking dish and sprinkle with the Kasseri
cheese. Bake for 30 to 40 minutes or until heated through. Serve with lamb or
grilled meats.

Note: This dish can be prepared in advance and stored, covered, in the
refrigerator. Bring it to room temperature and add the Kasseri cheese before baking.

Serves 8

Party Rice with Toasted Almonds

1/2 cup slivered almonds
2 cups (or more) chicken stock
1 cup uncooked long grain white rice
1 tablespoon butter
1 cup raisins and/or golden raisins
1 cup coarsely chopped dates
2 tablespoons butter

Preheat the oven to 350 degrees. Spread the almonds in a baking pan and toast until golden brown.

Bring the stock to a boil in a saucepan. Sauté the rice in 1 tablespoon butter in a large skillet over medium heat until golden brown. Add the stock and cover tightly. Simmer over low heat for 20 minutes, checking occasionally and adding additional chicken broth if needed.

Sauté the raisins and dates in 2 tablespoons butter in a medium sauté pan for 5 to 7 minutes. Add the fruit and almonds to the rice just before serving. Serve with grilled lamb chops or lamb shish kabobs.

Serves 6

Salt pork was popular in the original dish because the high salt content allowed it to be kept for long periods of time. The salting, drying, and curing process was accompanied by a slight fermentation that gave the pork a unique and pleasing flavor. Italian- and Spanish-cured hams and bacon have the same flavor. The Spanish or Mexicans sometimes use a smoked paprika, which you can approximate by toasting the paprika in a dry skillet for 1 to 2 minutes, taking care not to burn it. McCormick also markets a Spanish chili powder that works well and is not as hot as Hungarian hot paprika.

The Bells are Ringing
A CALL TO TABLE

131

Chile Rellenos Casserole

1 (16-ounce) can, or 4 (4-ounce) cans mild green chiles
1 pound Tillamook cheese, shredded
1 pound Monterey Jack cheese, shredded
5 egg yolks
1 (13-ounce) can evaporated milk
3 tablespoons all-purpose flour
1 teaspoon salt
5 egg whites

Preheat the oven to 350 degrees and spray a 9×13-inch baking dish with nonstick canola cooking spray. Layer the chiles, Tillamook cheese and Monterey Jack cheese in the prepared dish until all are used.

Beat the egg yolks with the evaporated milk, flour and salt in a bowl. Beat the egg whites in a mixing bowl until stiff peaks form. Fold into the egg yolk mixture. Pour over the layers. Bake for 1 hour. Serve with a variety of mild to hot salsas.

Note: You can cut this dish into 2-inch squares to serve as an appetizer.

Serves 10

Chiles from the Mission gardens, grown by the Mission's own "Gardening Angels."

Green Chile Salsa

4 or 5 Roma tomatoes, finely chopped
1 (7-ounce) can chopped green chiles
1 jalapeño chile, seeded and chopped, or
   to taste
1/3 cup minced sweet onion
1/3 cup chopped cilantro

juice of 1 lime
2 tablespoons olive oil
1/2 teaspoon cumin
1/2 teaspoon chili powder
salt and freshly ground pepper to taste

Combine the tomatoes, green chiles, jalapeño, onion, and cilantro in a medium bowl. Add the lime juice, olive oil, cumin, chili powder, salt and pepper and mix well. Serve with tortilla chips.

Serves 8

Tartar Sauce

2/3 cup sour cream
1/3 cup mayonnaise
2 teaspoons red wine vinegar
1 1/2 tablespoons creamy horseradish

1 1/2 tablespoons dill pickle relish
2 teaspoons sugar
seasoned salt and freshly ground pepper
   to taste

Combine the sour cream, mayonnaise and vinegar in a bowl. Stir in the horseradish, pickle relish, sugar, seasoned salt and pepper. Store in an airtight container in the refrigerator.

Makes 1 cup

Desserts

Sumptuous Delights to Crown the Meal

W hile the Mission's gardens offer tranquil retreat for visitors, their lovely ambience also provides a backdrop for festive annual celebrations, such as the Annual Mariachi Festival, the Lincoln Celebration, and "Christmas at the Mission" open house. Luncheons, garden shows, and educational programs are a few of the events hosted in the Central Courtyard.

Summer nights come magically alive with "Music Under the Stars" summer concert series and The Capistrano Valley Symphony concerts. The ultimate event hosted by the Mission is its "Annual Romance Gala," the black-tie fund-raising event coordinated by the Gala Committee and hosted by the Mission Preservation Foundation and The Ritz-Carlton, Laguna Niguel. Dining is always one of the important factors at these events.

In this section of the cookbook, readers will discover new recipes to delight the sweet tooth and add just the right touch to end any dining occasion.

Marble Cheesecake

Chocolate Crust

    1 (9-ounce) package chocolate wafers

    1/2 cup nuts

    1/4 cup (1/2 stick) butter, melted

    1/2 teaspoon ground cinnamon or nutmeg

Cheesecake

    4 ounces semisweet chocolate

    40 ounces cream cheese, softened

1^3/4 cups sugar

5 eggs

2 egg yolks

1/2 cup cream or heavy cream

5 tablespoons all-purpose flour

1 teaspoon vanilla extract or brandy

    For the crust, process the wafers and nuts in a food processor until crushed. Add the melted butter and cinnamon and process until smooth. Press over the bottom of a greased 12-inch springform pan.

    For the cheesecake, preheat the oven to 375 degrees. Melt the chocolate with a small amount of water in a saucepan. Let stand until cool.

    Combine the cream cheese with the sugar in a bowl and beat until light. Beat in the eggs, egg yolks, cream, flour and vanilla and beat until smooth. Pour into the crust. Dollop the chocolate over the top and swirl with a knife to marbleize. Bake for 1 hour and 20 minutes or until the center is firm. Let stand until cool. Place on a serving plate and remove the side of the pan. Store in the refrigerator until time to serve.

Serves 12 to 14

Demitasse Chocolate Dessert

8 ounces German's sweet chocolate

5 teaspoons water

2 egg yolks

2 teaspoons confectioners' sugar

1/2 cup chopped pecans

2 egg whites

1 cup heavy whipping cream

20 to 24 vanilla wafers

Combine the chocolate and water in a medium to large microwave-safe bowl. Microwave until the chocolate melts, stirring to blend well. Beat the egg yolks in a small bowl. Add the confectioners' sugar and pecans and mix well. Add to the chocolate and mix well.

Beat the egg whites in a bowl until stiff peaks form. Beat the cream in a bowl until soft peaks form. Fold the egg whites and then the whipped cream into the chocolate mixture.

Break one vanilla wafer into each demitasse cup. Spoon the chocolate into the cups and place one vanilla wafer upside down on the top of each. Garnish with additional whipped cream and a grating of additional chocolate.

Note: This can also be prepared in an 8×8-inch dish, breaking half the vanilla wafers into the bottom of the dish and topping the chocolate with the remaining wafers.

Serves 10 to 12

Chocolate Mint Dessert

4 ounces chocolate

1 cup (2 sticks) butter

2 cups confectioner's sugar

4 eggs

2 teaspoons vanilla extract

3/4 teaspoon peppermint extract

2 cups graham cracker crumbs

1/2 cup finely chopped walnuts

Melt the chocolate with the butter in a saucepan, stirring to blend well. Blend in the confectioners' sugar. Let stand until cool. Beat the mixture until light and fluffy. Beat in the eggs one at a time. Add the vanilla and peppermint extract and mix well.

Sprinkle some of the graham cracker crumbs into paper-lined muffin cups. Spoon the chocolate mixture into the cups and sprinkle with the remaining graham cracker crumbs and walnuts. Freeze until firm or for up to 1 week.

Remove to the refrigerator 30 minutes before serving. Peel off the paper liners and place the desserts on a serving tray. Garnish with a dollop of whipped cream.

Note: If you are concerned about using uncooked eggs, use eggs pasteurized in their shells, which are sold at some specialty food stores, or use an equivalent amount of pasteurized egg substitute.

Serves 12 to 16

Easy Chocolate Dessert

2 large milk chocolate with almonds candy bars
1 cup heavy whipping cream
16 vanilla wafers

Melt the chocolate bars in a double boiler over hot water. Let stand until cool. Whip the cream in a mixing bowl until soft peaks form. Fold in the melted chocolate. Place the vanilla wafers in a sealable plastic bag and roll with a rolling pin to crush into crumbs. Place three-fourths of the crumbs in an 8×8-inch glass dish. Pour the chocolate mixture over the crumbs. Sprinkle the top with the remaining crumbs. Chill for 8 to 10 hours before serving.

Serves 4 to 6

Egg Custard (Flan)

3/4 cup sugar
2 cups milk
2 cups light cream
6 eggs

1/2 cup sugar
2 teaspoons vanilla extract
1/2 teaspoon salt

Sprinkle 3/4 cup sugar in a skillet and cook over medium-high heat until caramelized to a light brown. Pour into a round baking dish, tilting the dish to coat the side.

Preheat the oven to 325 degrees. Combine the milk and cream in a saucepan over medium heat until bubbles form around the edge of the pan. Whisk together the eggs, 1/2 cup sugar, the vanilla and salt in a large bowl. Add the heated milk gradually, whisking constantly until smooth. Pour into the prepared baking dish.

Place the baking dish in a shallow pan and add enough boiling water to reach halfway up the side of the dish. Bake for 55 minutes or until a knife inserted in the center comes out clean.

Note: This can also be prepared in individual baking ramekins. Invert the ramekins onto dessert plates to serve.

Serves 6

Panna Cotta with Berry Sauce

1 cup milk

2 cups cream or heavy cream

1/2 vanilla bean

5 tablespoons fresh lemon juice

1 tablespoon unflavored gelatin

1/2 cup sugar

1 cup crème fraîche

2 tablespoons grated lemon zest

Berry Sauce (page 141)

Combine the milk and cream in a medium heavy saucepan. Split the vanilla bean lengthwise. Scrape the seeds into the milk mixture, and then add the bean. Bring just to a simmer and remove from the heat. Let stand, covered, for 30 minutes. Remove the vanilla bean.

Place the lemon juice into a small bowl and sprinkle the gelatin over the juice. Let stand until the gelatin softens. Stir the softened gelatin and sugar into the milk mixture. Cook over low heat for 2 minutes or until the sugar and gelatin dissolve. Remove from the heat. Whisk in the crème fraîche and lemon zest. Spoon into six 3/4-cup ramekins that have been lightly oiled. Chill for 6 hours or longer.

Run a small knife around the edge of each ramekin. Place the bottoms of the ramekins one at a time in a bowl of hot water for 45 seconds. Invert a plate on the top of each ramekin and invert the ramekins onto the plates, shaking gently to release the panna cotta. Serve with Berry Sauce.

Note: Panna Cotta is an eggless custard. Both the custard and the sauce can be prepared a day in advance and chilled until serving time. Crème fraîche is available at many supermarkets. If it is unavailable, you can heat 1 cup cream or heavy cream to 85 degrees, or lukewarm, and stir in 2 tablespoons buttermilk. Let stand, covered, in a draft-free place for 24 to 48 hours or until slightly thickened. Chill until time to use.

Serves 8

Berry Sauce

3 cups frozen blackberries, raspberries or strawberries (about 12 ounces)
3 tablespoons light brown sugar
1/4 cup crème de cassis (optional)

Thaw the berries, reserving any juices that accumulate. Combine 2 cups of the berries with the reserved juices, brown sugar and crème de cassis in a blender. Process until pureéd. Strain the mixture into a medium bowl, pressing the solids to remove as much liquid as possible; discard the solids. Stir in the remaining 1 cup berries. Store, covered, in the refrigerator.

Note: The crème de cassis, a black currant liqueur, goes especially well with blackberries.

Serves 8

Spring Blooms at the Mission

Merveilles

Combine 2 cups all-purpose flour, 1/2 cup sugar and 1/2 teaspoon salt in a bowl. Add 2 eggs, 1/2 cup (1 stick) melted butter, 2 tablespoons rum, 1 teaspoon water and 1/2 teaspoon vanilla and mix to form a dough. Roll on a floured surface into 12- to 15-inch pieces and cut into the desired shape. Deep-fry in heated vegetable oil until golden brown. Drain on paper towels and sprinkle with sugar.

*Recipe provided by
Mrs. Eugenie Oyharzabal*

The Bells are Ringing
A CALL TO TABLE

California Governor Schwarzenegger's Kaiserschmarren

This is a favorite Austrian recipe of California Governor Arnold Schwarzenegger and a treat that he enjoys with his family. Soak 2 tablespoons raisins in rum for 15 minutes; drain. Whisk 2 eggs and 1 egg white in a mixing bowl until foamy. Whisk in a pinch of salt and 1/4 cup all-purpose flour. Add 1 to 2 tablespoons milk or cream very gradually, whisking constantly to form a smooth batter. Stir in the raisins. Melt 1 tablespoon butter in a medium nonstick ovenproof skillet over medium heat. Add the batter and cook until golden brown on both sides, turning once.

continued ➤

Mascarpone Café Cream Dessert

6 large egg yolks

1 cup sugar

1 cup dry Marsala

2 tablespoons instant coffee granules

1 teaspoon hot water

24 ounces mascarpone cheese

12 ounces ladyfingers

1/2 cup dry Marsala

Add water to a depth of 3 inches in the bottom of a double boiler or a large saucepan and bring to a boil. Whisk the egg yolks with the sugar in a medium stainless steel mixing bowl or the top of a double boiler for 2 minutes or until pale yellow. Whisk in 1 cup wine. Place the bowl or double boiler over, but not touching, the boiling water and cook for 4 minutes, or to 160 degrees and until creamy and doubled in volume, whisking constantly. Remove from the heat. Dissolve the coffee granules in 1 teaspoon hot water in a cup. Stir the mixture into the egg yolk mixture. Add the mascarpone cheese and mix well.

Line the bottom of a 10-inch springform pan with baking parchment or waxed paper. Brush both sides of the ladyfingers with 1/2 cup wine. Arrange enough ladyfingers to cover the bottom of the pan in a daisy pattern, arranging them smooth side up and filling in all spaces. Cut the remaining ladyfingers into halves and arrange around the side of the pan with the cut side down and smooth side in.

Spoon the mascarpone mixture into the prepared pan. Chill, covered with plastic wrap, for 8 hours to 2 days. Invert the dessert onto a platter and remove the side and bottom of the pan; remove the parchment. Garnish with whipped cream and chocolate-covered coffee beans.

Serves 8 to 10

Mascarpone Cream

8 ounces mascarpone cheese
2 cups cream or heavy cream
1/4 cup sugar
1 teaspoon grated lemon zest

Combine the cheese, cream, sugar and lemon zest in a medium bowl and beat at medium speed for 1 to 2 minutes or until soft peaks form. Remove to a clean bowl and chill, covered, for up to 30 minutes. Serve with any dessert.

Serves 8 to 10

Bake at 400 degrees for 4 or 5 minutes or until slightly puffed. Tear into bite-size pieces with spatulas or wooden spoons and push to one side of the skillet. Return to medium heat and melt 1 tablespoon butter in the other side of the skillet. Sprinkle 2 tablespoons sugar over the butter and cook for 1 to 2 minutes or until bubbly. Toss the torn pancake pieces in the sugar mixture and remove to serving plates. Dust with confectioners' sugar and serve with cranberry sauce or berry preserves.

Reflecting Pond in the Central Courtyard

Apple Cobbler with Cheese Crust

8 cups sliced tart cooking apples

1/4 teaspoon salt

1 cup sugar

1/2 cup (1 stick) butter

1 cup sifted all-purpose flour

1 cup (4 ounces) shredded mild to very sharp
Cheddar cheese

1/2 cup sugar

1/2 teaspoon ground cinnamon

Preheat the oven to 350 degrees. Mix the apples with the salt and 1 cup sugar in a bowl. Place in a buttered shallow 2-quart baking pan. Cut the butter into the flour in a bowl. Add the cheese, 1/2 cup sugar and cinnamon and mix well. Pat a small amount at a time between your hands to form thin cakes. Place the cakes in an overlapping layer on the apples. Bake for 50 minutes or until the apples are tender and the crust is brown. Serve warm with whipped cream or ice cream.

Serves 6 to 8

Cranberry Apple Crisp

1 cup all-purpose flour

1 cup rolled oats

2/3 cup packed brown sugar

1/2 cup (1 stick) butter

9 large apples, peeled and sliced

2 cups fresh cranberries

1 cup granulated sugar

1 1/2 teaspoons ground cinnamon

6 tablespoons all-purpose flour

6 tablespoons butter, cut into pieces

Preheat the oven to 350 degrees. Mix 1 cup flour, the oats and brown sugar in a bowl. Cut in 1/2 cup butter until crumbly. Combine the apples and cranberries in a bowl and toss to mix. Mix the granulated sugar and cinnamon together. Layer the fruit, 6 tablespoons flour, 6 tablespoons butter and the cinnamon-sugar half at a time in a greased 9×13-inch baking pan, ending with the cinnamon-sugar. Sprinkle the oat mixture over the top. Bake for 1 hour.

Serves 8 to 10

Fruit Kuchen

1¹/₄ cups all-purpose flour

¹/₄ teaspoon salt

¹/₂ cup (1 stick) butter, chilled and
   cut into pieces

2 tablespoons sour cream

3 egg yolks

¹/₃ cup sour cream

¹/₄ cup all-purpose flour

1 cup sugar

¹/₄ teaspoon salt

fruit such as peaches, pears or apricots,
   peeled and thickly sliced

Preheat the oven to 375 degrees. Combine the flour, salt and butter in a food processor and process until crumbly. Add the sour cream and process until the mixture forms a ball. Press over the bottom and side of a medium tart pan with a removable bottom. Bake for 20 minutes or until light brown. Let stand until cool.

Reduce the oven temperature to 350 degrees. Combine the egg yolks, sour cream, flour, sugar and salt in a food processor and process for 5 seconds to form the custard. Pour half the custard into the crust. Arrange the fruit over the custard and spoon the remaining custard over the top.

Bake for 40 to 50 minutes or until the custard is set. Cool in the refrigerator. Place on a serving plate and garnish with mint leaves.

Note: This can be prepared 4 to 24 hours in advance and stored in the refrigerator until serving time.

Serves 8

Champagne Sorbet

2 cups club soda
1 cup sugar
1/2 cup orange juice
1/4 cup lemon juice
2 1/2 cups Champagne plus 2 tablespoons for topping

Combine the club soda, sugar, orange juice and lemon juice in a medium saucepan and mix well. Bring to a boil and reduce the heat. Cook until the sugar dissolves, stirring constantly. Chill, covered, in the refrigerator.

Stir 2 1/2 cups Champagne gently into the juice mixture. Pour into a 2-quart freezer container and freeze until firm. Scoop into six serving glasses and drizzle 1 teaspoon additional Champagne over each serving. Garnish the edges of the glasses with strawberries and mint leaves.

Serves 6

Fruit Sorbet

1 (28-ounce) can fruit, such as pears or peaches
2 cups fresh fruit, such as berries, grapefruit sections or
   chopped melon, mango or papaya
1 tablespoon lime juice or lemon juice

Process the undrained canned fruit in a food processor until puréed. Add the fresh fruit and lime juice and process until smooth. Spoon into a freezer container and freeze for 2 days or longer. Scoop into very small glasses and garnish with additional fruit, mint leaves or edible flowers. Serve as a palate cleanser between courses.

Serves 12 to 14

Papaya Baked Alaska

3 small papayas, cut into halves and seeded

1 quart coconut ice cream or vanilla ice cream

6 egg whites, at room temperature

1/2 teaspoon cream of tartar

1 cup sugar

1 teaspoon vanilla extract

3/4 cup flaked or shredded coconut

Preheat the oven to 500 degrees. Line a large baking sheet with heavy-duty foil. Place the papaya halves cut side up in the prepared pan. Beat the egg whites with the cream of tartar in a mixing bowl until soft peaks form. Add the sugar and vanilla gradually, beating constantly until stiff and glossy. Divide the ice cream among the six papaya halves, filling the cavities where the seeds were removed and mounding slightly. Completely cover the filled papayas with a thick coating of the meringue. Sprinkle each with the coconut. Bake on the center oven rack for 3 to 5 minutes or until the meringue is golden brown. Remove to serving plates with a large spatula and serve immediately.

Note: You may have to cut a small slice from the bottom of the papayas so they will sit flat on the baking sheet.

Serves 6

Sopaipillas

Mix 2 cups all-purpose flour, 1 tablespoon baking powder and 1/2 teaspoon salt in a bowl. Cut in 1 tablespoon shortening. Add 2/3 cup warm water gradually, mixing with a fork to form a dough. Knead for 3 to 5 minutes or until smooth. Divide into two portions and let stand, covered, for 10 minutes. Roll each portion into a 10×12 1/2-inch rectangle on a floured surface; cut each rectangle into twenty 2 1/2-inch squares with a fluted pastry wheel or knife. Heat vegetable oil to 425 degrees in a heavy 3-quart deep fryer. Add the pastry squares two at a time and fry for 30 seconds on each side or until golden brown. Drain on paper towels and sprinkle with confectioners' sugar. Serve warm or cool with honey.

The Bells are Ringing
A CALL TO TABLE

Easy Fruit Pizza

Orange Sauce

1/3 cup sugar

1 tablespoon cornstarch

salt to taste

1/2 cup orange juice

2 tablespoons lemon juice

1/4 cup water

Pizza

1 (18-ounce) package refrigerator sugar cookie dough

8 ounces cream cheese, softened

4 ounces whipped topping

fruit such as sliced strawberries, blueberries, raspberries and sliced kiwifruit

For the sauce, mix the sugar, cornstarch and salt in a saucepan. Blend in the orange juice, lemon juice and water. Bring to a boil and cook until thickened, stirring constantly. Let stand until cool.

For the pizza, preheat the oven to 350 degrees. Cut the cookie dough into slices 1/8 inch thick. Arrange in slightly overlapping concentric circles on a lightly greased large pizza pan, beginning 1/4 inch from the edge; press the edges together to seal. Bake for 8 to 10 minutes or just until the edge is light brown; do not overbake. Let stand until cool.

Blend the cream cheese with the whipped topping in a bowl. Spread over the cooled crust. Arrange fresh fruit in a decorative pattern over the cream cheese layer. Spoon the sauce over the fruit.

Note: You can substitute the fruit of your choice for the fruit suggested in the recipe.

Serves 8 to 10

Apple Hill Cake

Cake

- 2 cups all-purpose flour
- 2 teaspoons baking soda
- 2 teaspoons ground cinnamon
- 1 teaspoon nutmeg
- 1 teaspoon salt
- 2 cups sugar
- 1/2 cup vegetable oil
- 2 eggs, beaten
- 4 cups sliced apples
- 1/2 cup chopped nuts

Cream Cheese Frosting

- 8 ounces cream cheese, softened
- 1 tablespoon (or more) milk
- 1 teaspoon vanilla extract
- salt to taste
- 2 1/2 cups confectioners' sugar

For the cake, preheat the oven to 350 degrees. Sift the flour, baking soda, cinnamon, nutmeg and salt together. Combine the sugar, oil, eggs and apples in a mixing bowl and mix well. Add the dry ingredients and stir until moistened. Stir in the nuts.

Spread in a greased and floured 9×13-inch cake pan. Bake for 1 hour or until the cake tests done. Cool on a wire rack.

For the frosting, combine the cream cheese, milk, vanilla and salt in a mixing bowl and mix well. Add the confectioners' sugar gradually, beating constantly until smooth, adding additional milk if needed for the desired consistency. Spread over the cooled cake.

Note: You can serve the cake with whipped cream instead of the frosting if preferred.

Serves 12

Orange Slice Candy Fruitcake

1 teaspoon baking soda

1/2 cup buttermilk

1 (16-ounce) package orange slice candy

1 (8- to 10-ounce) package pitted
    dates, chopped

1 cup flaked coconut

2 cups chopped pecans

1/2 cup all-purpose flour

1 cup (2 sticks) butter, softened

2 cups sugar

4 eggs

1/2 teaspoon salt

3 cups all-purpose flour

Orange Glaze (page 151)

Preheat the oven to 325 degrees. Stir the baking soda into the buttermilk in a cup. Chop the candy by hand and mix with the dates, coconut and pecans in a bowl. Add 1/2 cup flour and toss to coat evenly.

Cream the butter and sugar in a mixing bowl until light and fluffy. Beat in the eggs one at a time. Add the buttermilk mixture and salt and mix well. Add 3 cups flour gradually, mixing well after each addition. Stir in the fruit and candy mixture.

Spoon into a tube pan sprayed with nonstick cooking spray. Bake for 1 hour. Reduce the oven temperature to 300 degrees and bake for 45 minutes longer.

Pour the Orange Glaze over the hot cake and let stand until cool. Chill, covered, in the refrigerator for 8 hours or longer. Invert onto a serving plate to serve.

Note: To prepare the cake in a bundt pan, bake at 300 degrees for 40 minutes. Reduce the oven temperature to 275 degrees and bake for 45 minutes longer, covering loosely with foil if necessary to prevent overbrowning. To prepare in three loaf pans, bake at 300 degrees for 1 1/2 hours, covering loosely with foil during the last 45 minutes if necessary to prevent overbrowning.

Serves 8 to 10

Orange Glaze

1 cup freshly squeezed orange juice
1 cup confectioners' sugar

Mix the orange juice and confectioners' sugar in a bowl. Use to glaze the Orange Slice Candy Fruitcake (page 150).

Serves 8 to 10

Mission Garden, Front Courtyard

Banana Pound Cake

2 very ripe bananas, mashed
1 (2-layer) package lemon cake mix
1/3 cup vegetable oil
2 eggs
1/2 cup chopped walnuts (optional)

Preheat the oven to 350 degrees. Combine the mashed bananas with enough water to measure 1 1/4 cups and mix until smooth. Combine the cake mix with the oil and eggs in a mixing bowl and mix until smooth. Add the banana mixture and walnuts and mix well.

Spoon into a greased and floured bundt pan and bake for 40 minutes or until the cake tests done. Invert onto a wire rack to cool. Glaze with a mixture of confectioners' sugar and lemon juice, if desired.

Serves 10 to 14

The Bells are Ringing
A CALL TO TABLE

Cranberry Pound Cake

Cake

2 cups all-purpose flour

1 cup sugar

2 teaspoons baking powder

salt to taste

2 eggs

3 tablespoons butter

1 cup heavy cream

2 cups fresh cranberries, chopped

Hot Butter Sauce

1/2 cup (1 stick) butter

1/2 cup heavy cream

1 cup sugar

1 teaspoon vanilla extract

For the cake, preheat the oven to 350 degrees. Mix the flour, sugar, baking powder and salt in a large mixing bowl. Add the eggs, butter, and cream and mix well. Stir in the cranberries. Spoon into a greased 10-inch bundt pan and bake for 40 minutes. Remove to a serving plate.

For the sauce, combine the butter, cream, sugar and vanilla in a double boiler. Cook over hot water until heated through. Serve warm over the cake.

Serves 8 to 10

Chocolate Torte

2 cups (12 ounces) chocolate chips
1 cup (2 sticks) butter
5 eggs
1¼ cups sugar
5 tablespoons all-purpose flour
1½ teaspoons baking powder

Preheat the oven to 325 degrees. Melt the chocolate chips with the butter in a saucepan, stirring to blend well. Set stand until cool.

Beat the eggs with the sugar, flour and baking powder in a mixing bowl. Add the chocolate mixture and mix well. Spread evenly in a buttered and floured cake pan. Bake for 30 minutes. Cover with foil and bake for 10 minutes longer or until the cake tests done but is still very moist. Chill in the refrigerator. Serve with ice cream and warm chocolate sauce.

Note: You may frost with your favorite chocolate frosting and garnish with almonds.

Serves 6 to 8

Sherry Poppy Seed Cake

1 (2-layer) package yellow cake mix
1 (4-ounce) package vanilla pudding mix
3/4 cup vegetable oil
3/4 cup water

4 eggs, beaten
1/2 cup sherry
1/3 cup poppy seeds
confectioners' sugar

Preheat the oven to 350 degrees. Combine the cake mix, pudding mix, oil, water, eggs, sherry and poppy seeds in a mixing bowl and mix well. Pour into a greased and floured bundt pan. Bake for 1 hour or until the cake tests done. Cool in the pan for a few minutes. Remove from the pan and sprinkle the warm cake with confectioners' sugar.

Serves 8 to 10

Almond Cookies

1 cup (2 sticks) unsalted butter, softened
2/3 cup sugar
1 egg
1/4 teaspoon vanilla extract
1/4 teaspoon almond extract

1/2 teaspoon salt
2 cups all-purpose flour
1/2 cup coarsely chopped almonds
confectioners' sugar or colored sugar

Cream the butter and sugar in a mixing bowl until light and fluffy. Beat in the egg, vanilla, almond extract and salt. Add the flour and almonds and mix to form a firm smooth dough. Shape into two logs or press into circles and wrap in plastic wrap. Chill for 2 hours or longer.

Preheat the oven to 375 degrees. Unwrap the dough and slice into thin rounds or cut with cookie cutters. Place on a cookie sheet lined with baking parchment. Bake for 10 to 12 minutes or until light golden brown. Let stand on the cookie sheet for several minutes and remove to a wire rack to cool completely. Sprinkle with confectioners' sugar or colored sugar.

Makes 2 dozen

Almond and Apricot Biscotti

2³/4 cups sifted all-purpose flour

1¹/2 cups sugar

2¹/2 teaspoons baking powder

1 teaspoon ground ginger

1 teaspoon salt

¹/2 cup (1 stick) unsalted butter, chilled and
   cut into pieces

6 ounces white chocolate, cut into pieces

1²/3 cups whole almonds, toasted

2 eggs

5 tablespoons apricot brandy

2 teaspoons almond extract

1 (6-ounce) package dried apricots, chopped

Combine the flour, sugar, baking powder, ginger, salt and butter in a food processor and process to a fine meal consistency. Add the white chocolate and process until finely chopped. Add the almonds and pulse six to eight times. Beat the eggs with the brandy and almond extract in a large mixing bowl. Add the flour mixture and apricots and mix to form a moist dough. Shape into two logs 2-inches in diameter on a 12×18-inch cookie sheet lined with baking parchment. Chill for 30 minutes or until firm.

Preheat the oven to 350 degrees. Bake the logs just until golden brown in color. Remove to a wire rack to cool completely. Reduce the oven temperature to 300 degrees. Cut the logs crosswise into ³/4-inch slices and arrange cut side down on the cookie sheet. Bake for 10 minutes. Turn the cookies and bake for 10 minutes longer. Remove to a wire rack to cool completely. Store in an airtight container for up to 2 weeks.

Note: For testing purposes, Lindt White Chocolate was used.

Makes 2 dozen

Cardamom Crisps

1/2 cup (1 stick) unsalted butter, softened
1/3 cup sugar
1 egg
1 teaspoon vanilla extract

2 teaspoons cardamom
1/8 teaspoon salt
3/4 cup all-purpose flour

Preheat the oven to 375 degrees. Cream the butter and sugar in a mixing bowl until light and fluffy. Beat in the egg, vanilla, cardamom and salt. Add the flour gradually, beating constantly until smooth.

Drop by teaspoonfuls 2 to 3 inches apart on a greased cookie sheet. Bake for 10 minutes or until the edges are golden brown. Cool on the cookie sheet for several minutes. Remove to a wire rack to cool completely.

Makes 3 dozen

Sliced Chocolate Walnut Cookies

1/2 cup (1 stick) butter, softened
3/4 cup sugar
1 egg
4 ounces chocolate, melted

1/2 teaspoon vanilla extract
13/4 cups all-purpose flour
1/4 teaspoon salt
3/4 cup walnuts, finely chopped

Cream the butter and sugar in a mixing bowl until light and fluffy. Add the egg, chocolate and vanilla and beat until smooth. Add the flour, salt and walnuts and mix well. Shape the dough into a log 11/2 inches in diameter. Wrap in plastic wrap and chill for 8 to 10 hours.

Preheat the oven to 350 degrees. Unwrap the dough and cut into slices. Place 2 inches apart on cookie sheets lined with baking parchment. Bake for 10 minutes.

Makes 4 dozen

The Late
Monsignor Paul Martin

Monsignor Martin was Mission Pastor from 1961 to 1970 and from 1976 to 2005. During those thirty-eight years, he was a living example of humility, love, selflessness, and abiding faith. His was an imposing figure, big and broad-shouldered, with large strong hands that were always ready to reach out to those in need. During his tenure, Monsignor Martin worked to preserve the Mission, specifically the stabilization of The Great Stone Church. He also founded the Mission Docent Society in 1981.

continued ➤

Monsignor Martin's Cocoa Fudge Cookies

2 cups sugar

1/4 cup baking cocoa

1 cup milk

salt to taste

1/2 cup peanut butter

2 tablespoons butter

1 (7-ounce) jar marshmallow creme

2 teaspoons vanilla extract

4 cups graham cracker crumbs

1/2 cup chopped nuts (optional)

Combine the sugar, baking cocoa, milk and salt in a saucepan and mix well. Cook to 234 to 240 degrees on a candy thermometer, soft-ball stage. Remove from the heat and stir in the peanut butter, butter, marshmallow creme and vanilla. Pour over the graham cracker crumbs and nuts in a large bowl and mix well. Drop by spoonfuls onto waxed paper and let stand until cool.

Makes 4 to 5 dozen

Cream Wafers

Wafers

1 cup (2 sticks) butter, softened
1/3 cup cream or heavy cream
2 cups sifted all-purpose flour
sugar

Cream Filling

1/4 cup (1/2 stick) butter, softened
1 cup confectioners' sugar
1 egg
1 teaspoon vanilla extract
several drops of red food coloring

For the wafers, combine the butter, cream and flour in a mixing bowl and mix to form a dough. Chill in the refrigerator for 1 hour.

Preheat the oven to 375 degrees. Roll the dough on a floured surface and cut into small circles; sprinkle with sugar. Arrange on a cookie sheet lined with baking parchment and prick with a fork. Bake for 7 to 9 minutes or just until golden brown; do not overbake. Cool on the cookie sheet for several minutes and remove to a wire rack to cool completely.

For the filling, combine the butter, confectioners' sugar, egg and vanilla in a mixing bowl and beat until smooth. Beat in the desired amount of food coloring. Spread the filling on the smooth sides of half the wafers and top with the remaining wafers.

Note: If you are concerned about using an uncooked egg, use an egg pasteurized in its shell, which can be found at some specialty food stores, or use an equivalent amount of pasteurized egg substitute.

Makes 2 dozen

When he was asked for a recipe contribution for this book, he was happy to oblige in spite of the illness that would take his life the same year. Along with the recipe he sent this short message penned in a frail hand: "My message: 'God is Love,' St. John the Evangelist, Msgr. Martin, 3/17/05."

Shortly after his death on October 2, 2005, The Orange County Register listed Monsignor Martin as one of the "100 People Who Shaped Orange County." It is notable that Father Junipero Serra is on the same list.

The Bells are Ringing
A CALL TO TABLE

Mission Lemon Bars

2 cups sifted all-purpose flour
1/2 cup confectioners' sugar
1/4 teaspoon salt
1 cup (2 sticks) butter, chilled
4 eggs
2 cups granulated sugar
1/3 cup fresh lemon juice
11/2 teaspoons grated lemon zest
1/4 cup all-purpose flour
1 teaspoon baking powder
confectioners' sugar

Preheat the oven to 350 degrees. Mix the flour, confectioners' sugar and salt in a medium to large mixing bowl. Add the butter and cut in with a pastry blender or two knives until the consistency of coarse meal. Press evenly over the bottom of a 9×13-inch baking pan. Bake for 20 minutes or until light brown. Cool for 10 to 15 minutes.

Beat the eggs in a large mixing bowl. Add the granulated sugar and beat until smooth. Beat in the lemon juice and lemon zest. Sift in the flour and baking powder and mix well. Spread evenly over the baked crust. Bake for 25 minutes. Cool in the pan on a wire rack. Sprinkle with confectioners' sugar and cut into small squares to serve. Store in an airtight container for 4 days or in the refrigerator for up to 11/2 weeks.

Makes 4 dozen

Chocolate Butterscotch Oatmeal Cookies

3 cups rolled oats

1 cup all-purpose flour

1 teaspoon baking soda

1 teaspoon salt

1 cup shortening or butter, melted

1 cup packed light brown sugar

1 cup granulated sugar

2 eggs

1 teaspoon vanilla extract

2 cups (12 ounces) chocolate chips

1 cup (6 ounces) butterscotch chips

Preheat the oven to 350 degrees. Mix the oats, flour, baking soda and salt together in medium bowl. Add the shortening, brown sugar, granulated sugar, eggs and vanilla and mix with a spoon. Stir in the chocolate chips and butterscotch chips.

Drop by tablespoonfuls or small ice cream scoopfuls onto a lightly greased or baking parchment-lined cookie sheet, leaving space for the cookies to spread. Bake for 15 minutes or until golden brown. Cool on the cookie sheet for 5 to 10 minutes and remove to a wire rack to cool completely.

Makes 2 to 3 dozen

The Bells are Ringing
A CALL TO TABLE

Flourless Peanut Butter Cookies

1 cup chunky or creamy peanut butter
1 cup packed light or dark brown sugar
1 egg
1 teaspoon baking soda
1 cup (6 ounces) chocolate chips

Preheat the oven to 350 degrees. Combine the peanut butter, brown sugar, egg and baking soda in a medium bowl and beat until smooth. Stir in the chocolate chips. Drop 2 inches apart onto an ungreased cookie sheet. Bake for 10 to 15 minutes or until puffed and light golden brown but still soft to the touch. Cool on the cookie sheet for 5 minutes and remove to a wire rack to cool completely.

Makes 2 dozen

The Bells are Ringing
A CALL TO TABLE

Pecan Pie Bars

1 1/4 cups all-purpose flour

3 tablespoons brown sugar

1/2 cup (1 stick) butter

2 eggs

1/2 cup packed brown sugar

1/2 cup light corn syrup

2 tablespoons butter, melted

1 teaspoon vanilla extract

1/2 cup chopped pecans

Preheat the oven to 375 degrees. Mix the flour and brown sugar in a bowl. Cut in the butter to form coarse crumbs. Press over the bottom of an ungreased 7×11-inch baking pan. Bake for 20 minutes.

Beat the eggs in a bowl. Stir in the brown sugar, corn syrup, butter, vanilla and pecans. Spread evenly over the hot crust. Bake for 15 to 20 minutes or until the center is set. Cool slightly. Cut into small bars and cool completely. Store, covered, in the refrigerator or freezer.

Makes 2 dozen

Prissy Pecans

2 tablespoons instant coffee granules

2 tablespoons water

1/4 cup sugar

1/4 teaspoon ground cinnamon

salt to taste

2 cups pecans halves

Combine the instant coffee granules, water, sugar, cinnamon and salt in a saucepan and mix well. Stir in the pecans. Bring to a boil over medium heat and cook for 3 minutes, stirring constantly. Spread on release-type foil and let stand, separating with forks as the pecans cool.

Makes 2 cups

The Bells are Ringing
A CALL TO TABLE

Charles Lummis and the Landmarks Club

Newsman Charles Fletcher Lummis was a staunch activist on behalf of historic preservation. After his arrival in California, Lummis established the Landmarks Club in 1895 to preserve California's Spanish missions. One of the first projects focused on the Mission San Juan Capistrano, and one of Lummis's fundraising efforts was the compilation and sale of a cookbook for five cents a copy. He appointed Judge Richard Egan, a prominent and colorful figure in San Juan Capistrano, to survey and oversee the reconstruction work at the Mission, saving the Mission from hopeless ruin.

continued ➤

Easy Sugar Cookies

3 cups sifted all-purpose flour	1 cup sugar
1/2 teaspoon salt	2 egg yolks
1 teaspoon baking powder	1 teaspoon vanilla extract
1 cup (2 sticks) butter, softened	1/2 cup milk

Mix the flour, salt and baking powder together. Cream the butter and sugar in a mixing bowl until light and fluffy. Mix the egg yolks and vanilla together and beat into the creamed mixture. Add the flour mixture and milk and mix well. Chill the dough until firm enough to handle or until ready to roll out.

Preheat the oven to 350 degrees. Roll the dough into a circle on a lightly floured surface. Cut into desired shapes and place 2 inches apart on cookie sheets lined with parchment paper. Bake until light brown around the edges. Remove to a wire rack to cool. Frost with your favorite confectioners' sugar icing.

Makes about 4 to 5 dozen

Mission Bell Wall or Campanario

Berry Cream Tart

Graham Cracker Crust

26 graham crackers

2 tablespoons sugar

2 tablespoons butter, melted

4 teaspoons water

Cheese Filling

2/3 cup Neufchâtel cheese,
softened

1/4 cup sugar

1/2 teaspoon vanilla extract

1/4 teaspoon almond extract

Strawberry Topping

6 cups fresh strawberries,
raspberries or blueberries

2/3 cup sugar

1 tablespoon cornstarch

1 tablespoon lemon juice

2 tablespoons sliced
almonds, toasted

For the crust, preheat the oven to 350 degrees. Process the graham crackers to crumbs in a food processor. Add the sugar, butter and water and pulse just until moistened. Press over the bottom and 3/4 inch up the side of a 9-inch tart pan sprayed with nonstick cooking spray. Bake for 10 minutes or until light brown. Cool on a wire rack.

For the filling, combine the Neufchâtel cheese, sugar, vanilla and almond extract in a medium mixing bowl and beat until smooth. Spread over the cooled crust.

For the topping, process 2 cups of the strawberries in a food processor until puréed. Combine the purée with the sugar, cornstarch and lemon juice in a small saucepan and mix well. Bring to a boil over medium heat, whisking constantly. Reduce the heat and cook for 1 minute longer or until thickened, whisking constantly. Spoon into a bowl and cool.

Spread half the strawberry glaze over the filling. Arrange the remaining 4 cups strawberries bottoms up in a circular pattern over the filling. Spoon the remaining strawberry glaze over the berries. Sprinkle the almonds around the edge. Chill, covered, for 3 hours.

Serves 10

The Mission today is alive with visitors from all over the world. Children are wide-eyed and curious about the place and are taught the history of California and the missions by docents and living history volunteers. Artists gather to paint the Mission and record its many faces for posterity. Magnificent musical events are held under the stars. One might suppose that Padre Junipero Serra—and Charles Lummis—would be proud.

Orange Cranberry Tart

Almond Crust

    1 cup slivered almonds

    1/2 cup (1 stick) butter

    3 tablespoons brown sugar

    1 egg

    1 1/2 cups all-purpose flour

Tart

    1 envelope unflavored gelatin

    1/4 cup orange juice

    2/3 cup orange marmalade

    1/2 to 3/4 cup packed brown sugar

    4 1/2 cups fresh cranberries

    1/3 cup marmalade

For the crust, grind the almonds in a food processor. Add the butter, brown sugar, egg and 1 cup of the flour; process until the mixture forms a ball. Add the remaining 1/2 cup flour and process to form a dough. Press over the bottom and 2 inches up the side of a 9- or 10-inch springform pan. Chill for 20 minutes.

Preheat the oven to 350 degrees. Bake the crust for 20 minutes or until the edge is golden brown. Cool on a wire rack.

For the tart, sprinkle the gelatin over the orange juice in a saucepan and let stand until softened. Stir in 2/3 cup marmalade and the brown sugar. Bring to a boil and stir in the cranberries. Reduce the heat and simmer, covered, for 10 minutes. Remove from the heat and skim off any foam. Spoon into the cooled crust. Chill for several hours.

Place the tart on a serving plate and remove the side of the pan. Melt 1/3 cup marmalade in a saucepan and brush over the top of the tart.

Note: This is a beautiful holiday dessert.

Serves 8

Citrus Tart

Pâte Sucrée

  1½ cups all-purpose flour

  1½ tablespoons sugar

  ½ cup (1 stick) unsalted butter, chilled and
    cut into pieces

  1 egg yolk, lightly beaten

  2 tablespoons ice water

Tart

  1 tablespoon grated orange zest
    (about 1 orange)

  1 tablespoon grated lemon zest
    (about 1 lemon)

  Zest of 2 lemons (1 tablespoon)

  ½ cup freshly squeezed orange juice

  ½ cup freshly squeezed lemon juice

  ¾ cup sugar

  6 tablespoons crème fraîche or sour cream

  6 eggs

  ½ cup orange marmalade with long strips of
    orange zest

For the pâte sucrée, pulse the flour and sugar in a food processor to combine. Add the butter and pulse for 15 seconds or until the mixture resembles coarse meal. Lightly beat the egg yolk with the ice water. Add to the flour mixture in a slow steady stream, processing constantly until the dough just holds together. Press the dough into a flat disk on a piece of plastic wrap. Chill for 1 hour.

Roll the pâte sucrée ⅛ inch thick on a lightly floured surface. Place in the bottom of a 9-inch tart pan with a removable bottom and chill for 30 minutes. Preheat the oven to 375 degrees. Remove the pastry from the refrigerator and place on a baking sheet. Prick the pastry all over with a fork and then line carefully with parchment paper, pressing into the corners and edges. Weigh the pastry down with uncooked dried beans. Bake for 20 minutes. Remove the parchment paper and beans. Bake for 10 minutes longer or until the pastry is light golden brown. Cool on a wire rack for 15 minutes. Maintain the oven temperature.

For the tart, whisk the orange zest, lemon zest, orange juice, lemon juice and sugar in a medium bowl. Whisk in the crème fraîche until blended. Add the eggs and whisk until blended. Pour into the cooled pastry crust. Return to the oven and bake for 25 to 30 minutes or until the filling is set. Do not brown. Cool to room temperature on a wire rack. Heat the marmalade in a small saucepan over low heat until melted. Remove from the heat and let stand to cool for a few minutes. Spread evenly over the cooled tart. Serve at room temperature or chilled.

Serves 6 to 8

The "King" of Capistrano and the Santa Fe Railroad

Judge Richard Egan, sometimes referred as the "King" of Capistrano, was a prominent and colorful figure in the history of San Juan Capistrano, gaining popularity with the local residents in the late 1860s. He had a keen intellect, with the ability to understand and give legal advice to residents regarding California laws. He held the office of justice of the peace for more than fifty years. In addition to his Mission restoration work as a member of the Landmark Club, Judge Egan was instrumental in convincing the Santa Fe Railroad to run its tracks right through the center of town.

continued ➤

The Bells are Ringing
A CALL TO TABLE

Pumpkin Cream Cheese Tart

Graham Cracker Crust

1¹/₂ cups graham cracker crumbs

6 tablespoons butter, melted

¹/₄ cup sugar

Tart

40 ounces cream cheese, softened

1¹/₄ cups sugar

4 eggs

3 egg yolks

3 tablespoons all-purpose flour

2¹/₂ teaspoons ground cinnamon

1¹/₂ teaspoons ground cloves

1¹/₂ teaspoons ground ginger

¹/₂ cup heavy cream or cinnamon-flavored cream

1 (16-ounce) can pumpkin

2 tablespoons vanilla extract

For the crust, preheat the oven to 350 degrees. Combine the graham cracker crumbs, butter and sugar in a bowl and mix well. Press over the bottom and up the side of a 10-inch springform pan. Bake for 5 to 8 minutes or until golden brown.

For the tart, increase the oven temperature to 425 degrees. Beat the cream cheese with the sugar in a mixing bowl until light and fluffy. Beat in the eggs, egg yolks, flour, cinnamon, cloves and ginger. Add the cream, pumpkin and vanilla and mix well.

Spoon into the crust and bake for 15 minutes. Reduce the oven temperature to 325 degrees and bake for 1 hour longer or until the center is set. Cool on a wire rack. Place on a serving plate and remove the side of the pan.

Serves 12

Pecan Meringue Torte

3 egg whites
1/4 teaspoon cream of tartar
1/8 teaspoon salt
1 cup sugar

1 teaspoon vanilla extract
1 cup graham cracker crumbs
1 cup chopped pecans
sliced fruit

Preheat the oven to 350 degrees. Beat the egg whites in a mixing bowl until frothy. Add the cream of tartar and salt. Beat until stiff peaks form. Add the sugar 2 tablespoons at a time, beating until glossy after each addition. Beat in the vanilla. Fold in the graham cracker crumbs and pecans. Spread evenly in a lightly greased 9-inch baking pan. Bake for 20 to 30 minutes or until light brown. Serve with ice cream and top with sliced fruit.

Serves 6

Buttery Two-Crust Pie Pastry

3 cups all-purpose flour
1/4 cup sugar
salt to taste
2 egg yolks

1 cup (2 sticks) unsalted butter,
    frozen and cut into small pieces
1/2 teaspoon vanilla extract
4 to 6 tablespoons cold water

Mix the flour, sugar and salt in a food processor and pulse 5 or 6 times. Add the egg yolks, butter and vanilla and process for 10 seconds or to the consistency of coarse crumbs. Add enough water gradually to form a ball, processing constantly; do not overmix. Wrap in plastic wrap or place in a plastic bag and chill for 2 hours before using.

Note: This will make enough for one large two-crust or two large one-crust pies. Cover the crust loosely with foil during the baking time to prevent overbrowning.

Makes one 2-crust pie

The opening of the Capistrano Depot in 1887 changed the town of San Juan Capistrano forever. Farm products and livestock could be shipped to markets that were previously inaccessible. The tourist industry emerged, and visitors arrived with currency and cameras, easels and canvases on which to capture the beauty of the Mission. Travel to the town and Mission by train is still possible today, with regularly scheduled stops at the old Depot, now the home of Sarducci's and Rendevous restaurants.

The Bells are Ringing
A CALL TO TABLE

The Spirit of Hospitality

Throughout its history, Mission San Juan Capistrano has radiated a welcoming spirit of hospitality. Franciscan padres opened the Mission doors to weary travelers. Guests were welcomed, especially those who had come a distance and had news of the outside world to share. Travelers were offered the Mission's best food, wine, warm sleeping quarters, and respite.

In this chapter the bells ring out in glory and celebration. Readers will discover recipes for unique appetizers and beverages to share with family and friends (and the weary traveler) at parties, fiestas, and special gatherings.

Mission San Juan Capistrano and the Swallows

Mission San Juan Capistrano is known worldwide for its yearly return of the swallows from Goya, Argentina. Although they are not nearly as numerous now as they were in Father O'Sullivan's time, they do return, and their return is celebrated with gusto. On March 19, the Mission bells joyously proclaim the first sightings of the swallows as they return.

Blue Crab Imperial

2 tablespoons butter
1/4 cup all-purpose flour
2 cups milk
1 tablespoon Old Bay seasoning
1/2 teaspoon dry mustard
1 teaspoon salt
1/8 teaspoon pepper
1 egg yolk, beaten
2 tablespoons sherry
1 cup fresh bread crumbs
1 (6-ounce) can crab meat, drained
   and flaked
1 tablespoon butter, melted
1/2 cup fresh bread crumbs
paprika or cayenne pepper to taste

Preheat the oven to 400 degrees. Melt 2 tablespoons butter in a saucepan and blend in the flour. Cook until bubbly, stirring frequently. Add the milk gradually with the Old Bay seasoning, dry mustard, salt and pepper and cook until thickened, stirring constantly. Stir a small amount of the hot mixture into the egg yolk, then stir the egg yolk into the hot mixture. Cook for 2 minutes longer, stirring constantly.

Remove from the heat and stir in the sherry, 1 cup bread crumbs and the crab meat. Spoon into a greased baking dish. Toss 1 tablespoon melted butter with 1/2 cup bread crumbs in a bowl and sprinkle over the crab mixture. Sprinkle with paprika. Bake for 20 to 25 minutes or until heated through.

Serves 8

Hot Crab Meat Appetizer

8 ounces cream cheese, softened
1 tablespoon milk
1 (6-ounce) can crab meat, drained and flaked
2 tablespoons finely chopped or grated onion
1/4 teaspoon salt
pepper to taste
1/3 cup sliced or slivered almonds

Preheat the oven to 375 degrees. Beat the cream cheese with the milk in a mixing bowl until smooth. Add the crab meat, onion, salt and pepper and mix well. Spoon into a shallow 8-inch baking pan and sprinkle with the almonds. Bake for 15 minutes or until bubbly. Serve with assorted crackers.

Serves 8

St. Joseph's Day marks the annual return of the Swallows.

When the Swallows Come Back to Capistrano
by Leon René

Inspired by a live radio broadcast celebrating the annual return of the swallows to Mission San Juan Capistrano on March 19, songwriter Leon René sat at his desk in 1939 and penned the famous song, "When the Swallows Come Back to Capistrano." The song has since been recorded by twelve different artists, including The Ink Spots, Gene Autry, The King Sisters, and Anne Murray. It remained for weeks on top of "The Hit Parade" radio program. In the fall of 2005 the song was performed beautifully within the ruins of the Great Stone Church by recording artist and pianist, Michael Feinstein.

The Bells are Ringing
A CALL TO TABLE

Spicy Shrimp

3 tablespoons freshly grated ginger

4 teaspoons minced garlic

2 tablespoons sugar

1 tablespoon peanut oil or olive oil

1/4 cup sherry or dry vermouth

2 tablespoons sesame oil

2 tablespoons rice vinegar

1 teaspoon red chile paste

1/2 teaspoon Chinese five-spice powder

1/2 teaspoon red pepper flakes

1 1/2 pounds large shrimp, cooked, peeled and deveined

Sauté the ginger, garlic and sugar in the peanut oil in a saucepan. Add the sherry, sesame oil, vinegar, red chile paste, five-spice powder and red pepper flakes; mix well. Bring to a boil and remove from the heat. Add the shrimp and mix to coat well. Spoon into a glass bowl. Marinate, covered, in the refrigerator for 8 hours or longer.

Remove the shrimp to a platter with a slotted spoon. Garnish with thinly sliced lime and lemon. Serve as an appetizer or on a bed of mixed greens as a first course.

Serves 6

Salmon and Cucumber Rounds

1 large English cucumber
8 ounces whipped herb-flavor cream cheese
1¹/₂ pounds smoked salmon
20 to 30 capers

Score the peel of the cucumber lengthwise with the tines of a fork. Cut the cucumber into ¹/₄- to ¹/₂-inch slices, discarding the ends. Spread the cream cheese on the cucumber slices. Cut the salmon into ¹/₄- to ¹/₂-inch-wide strips. Roll the salmon strips, leaving a small space in the center of each roll; place a caper in each center space. Place the rolls seam side down on the cream cheese. Arrange on a serving tray lined with curly greens and garnish with lemon twists.

Makes 20 to 30

Avocado-Stuffed Eggs

6 hard-cooked eggs
3 tablespoons mayonnaise
3 slices bacon, crisp-cooked and crumbled
1 tablespoon prepared mustard
¹/₄ teaspoon paprika
salt to taste
1 ripe avocado, finely chopped

Cut the hard-cooked eggs into halves and remove the yolks to a small bowl. Add the mayonnaise to the egg yolks and mash well. Add the bacon, mustard, paprika and salt and mix well. Fold in the avocado. Fill the egg whites with the avocado mixture. Place on a tray lined with shredded lettuce. Garnish the tops of the eggs with parsley and/or sliced stuffed green olives.

Makes 12

The Bells are Ringing
A CALL TO TABLE

Feta Cheese Cups

8 slices firm white bread
1/4 cup (1/2 stick) butter, melted
1 large egg, beaten
3 ounces cream cheese, softened
1/4 cup crumbled feta cheese

Preheat the oven to 350 degrees. Cut each bread slice into three rounds with a 2-inch cutter. Brush one side of the bread with the melted butter and fit each round buttered side down into a greased miniature muffin cup.

Combine the egg, cream cheese and feta cheese in a bowl and mix until smooth. Drop one teaspoonful into each bread cup. Bake for 20 minutes or until puffed and light brown.

Note: These can be prepared in advance and baked at serving time.

Makes 24

The Bells are Ringing
A CALL TO TABLE

Spinach-Stuffed Mushrooms

1 cup cooked chopped spinach

16 large mushrooms, 2 to 2 1/2 inches
   in diameter

1/4 cup (1/2 stick) butter

1/2 cup dry bread crumbs

1 tablespoon chopped fresh parsley

1 tablespoon grated onion

few drops of Tabasco sauce, or to taste

1 teaspoon salt

1 teaspoon freshly ground pepper

2 eggs, beaten

melted butter

1/2 cup (2 ounces) grated Parmesan cheese

1 chicken bouillon cube

3/4 cup boiling water

Preheat the oven to 375 degrees. Squeeze any excess moisture from the spinach. Remove the stems from the mushrooms and finely chop. Wipe the mushroom caps with a damp cloth. Sauté the chopped mushroom stems in 1/4 cup butter in a skillet. Add the spinach, bread crumbs, parsley, onion, Tabasco sauce, salt and pepper. Remove from the heat to cool. Stir in the beaten eggs thoroughly.

Brush the bottom of a shallow baking dish with melted butter. Brush the mushroom caps with melted butter inside and out. Stuff each mushroom cap with the spinach mixture and place in the prepared dish. Sprinkle the cheese evenly over the mushrooms. Dissolve the bouillon cube in the boiling water in a small bowl. Pour into the bottom of the dish to keep the mushrooms from sticking. Bake for 20 to 30 minutes or until the mushrooms are brown and tender, drizzling with additional melted butter, if desired.

*Note: You may use 1 cup flaked crab meat or chopped shrimp instead of the spinach and add
1 teaspoon chopped fresh dill weed or tarragon.*

Serves 4

Roasted Asparagus with Prosciutto

1/4 cup goat cheese, boursin, or softened cream cheese
20 small thin slices prosciutto
20 asparagus spears, trimmed (about 1 pound)

Preheat the oven to 400 degrees. Spread a thin layer of the goat cheese on each slice of prosciutto. Place one asparagus spear on each slice of prosciutto and roll to enclose the asparagus. Place on a baking sheet sprayed with nonstick cooking spray. Roast for 15 minutes. Cool slightly before serving. Serve as an appetizer or side dish.

Makes 20

Oven-Roasted Tomatoes

12 round tomatoes or Roma tomatoes
coarse salt to taste
olive oil
herbes de Provence, dried rosemary or other dried herb of choice (optional)

Preheat the oven to 325 degrees. Cut the round tomatoes into halves crosswise or Roma tomatoes into halves lengthwise. Discard the seeds and juice. Place cut side up on a foil-lined baking sheet; sprinkle with coarse salt and drizzle with olive oil. Sprinkle with herbes de Provence. Roast for 2 1/2 to 3 hours or until done to taste. Serve as an appetizer with Roasted Asparagus with Prosciutto (above), with roasted meats, in pasta sauce or on pizza.

Makes 24

Smoked Salmon Cheese Ball

1 (14-ounce) can salmon, or 1 (12-ounce) can tuna
8 ounces cream cheese, softened
2 tablespoons creamy horseradish, or to taste
1 teaspoon liquid smoke, or to taste
$1/2$ tablespoon lemon juice
$1/4$ teaspoon garlic powder
salt to taste
chopped walnuts or parsley

Drain and flake the salmon, discarding the skin and bones. Combine the salmon with the cream cheese, horseradish, liquid smoke, lemon juice, garlic powder and salt in a bowl and mix well. Shape into a ball and roll in the walnuts. Place on a serving plate and garnish with parsley.

Serves 12 to 16

Pineapple Cheese Ball

1 (8-ounce) can crushed pineapple, drained
16 ounces cream cheese, softened
$1/2$ cup (2 ounces) shredded Cheddar cheese
2 tablespoons minced green bell pepper
2 tablespoons minced sweet onion
1 teaspoon seasoned salt
$1/2$ cup chopped nuts

Combine the pineapple, cream cheese, Cheddar cheese, bell pepper, onion and seasoned salt in a bowl and mix well. Shape into a ball and coat with the nuts, pressing the nuts lightly into the surface. Chill, covered, until firm. Place on a serving plate.

Serves 10 to 12

The Bells are Ringing
A CALL TO TABLE

The Serra Chapel

The most historically significant building of the Mission San Juan Capistrano is its Serra Chapel, the only known remaining church where Father Junipero Serra celebrated Mass. The Chapel's history has been marked by periods of neglect and was used as a storeroom during its secular period. In the 1920s, Father St. John O'Sullivan labored at its restoration.

continued ➤

Cheese and Olive Dip

4 ounces Cheddar cheese, shredded

4 ounces mozzarella cheese, shredded

2 (2-ounce) cans sliced black olives, drained

1 (6-ounce) jar green olives, drained and sliced

1/2 green bell pepper, finely chopped

6 green onions, finely chopped (white part and some of the green part)

1 cup mayonnaise

1 cup chopped pecans

Preheat the oven to 350 degrees. Combine the Cheddar cheese, mozzarella cheese, black olives, green olives, bell pepper, green onions and mayonnaise in a bowl and mix well. Spoon into a 9-inch shallow baking dish. Bake until the cheeses are melted. Sprinkle the pecans over the top. Serve warm with tortilla chips or crisp crackers.

Serves 6 to 8

The Serra Chapel, circa 2005. Appreciation is extended to William Lyon Holmes, Inc. for helping to underwrite the photographs in this book.

Tapenade

1 cup oil-cured black olives or
    kalamata olives, pitted
3 garlic cloves
2 tablespoons lemon juice
1 tablespoon chopped
    fresh parsley

1 teaspoon capers, drained
1/2 teaspoon Dijon mustard
1/2 teaspoon fresh thyme or
    dried thyme
1/2 cup extra-virgin olive oil

Process the olives, garlic, lemon juice, parsley, capers, Dijon mustard and thyme in a food processor until finely chopped but not puréed. Spoon into a serving bowl. Stir in the olive oil until well combined. Serve immediately or cover and chill in the refrigerator. Stir the mixture just before serving and garnish with sprigs of fresh thyme. Serve with toasted French baguette slices or sturdy but not heavily seasoned crackers.

Serves 6 to 8

Chutney and Cheese Spread

1/2 cup chutney
8 ounces cream cheese, softened
2 cups (8 ounces) shredded sharp
    Cheddar cheese

2 tablespoons chopped fresh
    chives or dried chives
1/2 cup finely chopped walnuts

Combine the chutney, cream cheese, Cheddar cheese and chives in a food processor and process until smooth. Spoon into a serving dish and sprinkle with the walnuts. Serve with crackers or toasted bread rounds.

Note: This recipe was tested using Major Gray's Chutney.

Makes 2 cups

His crowning joy was the great altar or golden retablo, an antique piece brought from Barcelona and given to him for Serra Chapel by the Bishop of Los Angeles. It was placed there in 1922. No visit to Mission San Juan Capistrano would be complete without seeing this beautiful, quaint, and tranquil chapel. The Mission Preservation Foundation initiated the Conservation of Serra Chapel Project in October of 2005. It is a three-year preservation project, with a budget of one and one-half million dollars to return the Chapel to its glory of the 1920s.

The Bells are Ringing
A CALL TO TABLE

Frosted Liverwurst Pâté

1 pound liverwurst

1 cup minced onion

1 garlic clove, crushed

1/2 teaspoon minced basil

8 ounces cream cheese, softened

1 teaspoon mayonnaise

1 garlic clove, crushed

1/8 teaspoon Tabasco sauce

Mash the liverwurst with a fork in a bowl. Add the onion, 1 garlic clove and basil and mix well. Shape into a smooth mound on a serving plate. Chill in the refrigerator. Blend the cream cheese, mayonnaise, 1 garlic clove and Tabasco sauce in a bowl. Spread over the chilled liverwurst mixture. Chill for 8 hours or longer. Garnish with parsley to serve.

Serves 12 to 16

Spinach Artichoke Dip

1 (10-ounce) package frozen chopped spinach

1 (6-ounce) jar marinated artichoke hearts

1 cup (4 ounces) grated Parmesan cheese

1 cup mayonnaise

1 (4-ounce) can diced green chiles

Preheat the broiler to high. Thaw the spinach; drain well. Drain the artichoke hearts and chop coarsely. Mix the cheese, mayonnaise, green chiles, spinach and artichoke hearts in a bowl. Spoon the mixture into a medium shallow baking dish. Broil for several minutes or until the top is golden brown. Serve with thin crackers or tortilla strips.

Serves 6 to 8

Toasted Almond Dip

8 ounces cream cheese, softened

1/3 cup mayonnaise-type salad dressing

1 1/2 cups (6 ounces) shredded Swiss cheese

2 tablespoons finely chopped green onions

1/8 teaspoon nutmeg

1/8 teaspoon pepper

1/3 cup toasted sliced almonds

Preheat the oven to 350 degrees. Combine the cream cheese, salad dressing, Swiss cheese, green onions, nutmeg and pepper in a bowl and mix well. Spread in a 9-inch baking dish. Bake for 15 minutes. Sprinkle with the almonds.

Note: This can be prepared in advance and chilled until baking time. Allow 5 to 8 minutes additional time for baking.

Serves 8

Blue Cheese and Shrimp Spread

6 ounces blue cheese, chilled

3/4 cup (1 1/2 sticks) butter, softened

1 tablespoon prepared mustard

2 teaspoons brandy

6 ounces finely chopped cooked shrimp

Combine the cheese, butter, mustard and brandy in a mixing bowl and beat until smooth and creamy. Add the shrimp and mix well. Spoon into a serving bowl. Chill, covered, in the refrigerator. Remove from the refrigerator 30 minutes before serving to soften. Serve with crisp crackers.

Serves 6 to 8

John Wayne's Southwest Dip

1 pound ground beef

1 pound bulk pork sausage

1 onion, finely chopped

5 to 6 ounces Velveeta cheese, cut into cubes

1 (28-ounce) can refried beans

1 (8-ounce) can tomato sauce

1 (5-ounce) bottle taco sauce

1 tablespoon chili powder

Cook the ground beef and sausage with the onion in a skillet, stirring until brown and crumbly; drain. Combine with the cheese, beans, tomato sauce, taco sauce and chili powder in a slow cooker. Cook on High until the cheese melts. Reduce the temperature to Low and serve with assorted chips.

Serves 12 to 14

Best Margaritas

1 (6-ounce) can frozen limeade concentrate, thawed

6 ounces tequila

6 ounces beer

Fill a blender $2/3$ full with crushed ice. Add the limeade concentrate, tequila and beer and blend until frothy. Serve in margarita glasses.

Serves 6

Sidecar

1 cup Cointreau
1/2 cup Triple Sec
juice of 1 orange

Combine the Cointreau, Triple Sec and orange juice in a cocktail shaker and chill in the refrigerator. Serve in martini glasses with edges that have been dipped in lemon juice and then into sugar to coat. Add crushed ice, if desired.

Makes 2 cups

Pink Lady

1 1/2 ounces gin
1 1/2 ounces cream or heavy cream
dash of grenadine

Combine the gin, cream and grenadine in a cocktail shaker. Add ice and shake to chill. Pour into a Champagne flute to serve.

Serves 1

The Hollywood Connection

As the Hollywood movie industry began to blossom in the early twentieth century, site scouts were drawn to the Mission and the town of San Juan Capistrano. In 1910, Mary Pickford appeared in a movie entitled "The Two Brothers," which was filmed on the Mission grounds and in surrounding areas. The film is presented occasionally by the San Juan Capistrano Historical Society.

continued ➤

Orange Sangria

1 orange
1/2 cup sugar
juice of 2 limes
2 cups fresh orange juice
1 (750-milliliter) bottle dry red wine
1/2 cup Cointreau or Triple Sec

Cut the orange into halves. Cut several thin slices from one half and reserve for the garnish. Remove a thin layer of the outer peel of the other orange half with a vegetable peeler. Combine the peel with the sugar in a bowl and bruise with the back of a spoon to release the oils. Add the lime juice, orange juice, wine and orange liqueur. Pour into a pitcher and chill, covered, in the refrigerator, removing the orange peel after 15 minutes. Garnish with the orange slices and serve over ice, if desired.

Makes 6 cups

Champagne Punch

juice of 2 oranges
juice of 2 lemons
$1/2$ cup sugar
1 cup unsweetened pineapple juice
$1/2$ cup white rum
$1/2$ cup dark rum
2 (750-milliliter) bottles Champagne, chilled

Combine the orange juice, lemon juice and sugar in a large punch bowl, stirring to dissolve the sugar. Add the pineapple juice, white rum, dark rum and Champagne and mix well. Add ice and serve immediately.

Serves 20

Mary Pickford later married at the Mission, and a painting of this event is included in the collection of paintings owned by the Mission. In 1927, another film called "Rose of the Golden West," was filmed there, starring Mary Astor. Other notable celebrity visitors to the Mission include President Richard M. Nixon, Marilyn Monroe, and Clint Eastwood. The Mission continues to serve as a filming and photography location for entertainment purposes.

Mary Pickford's Wedding by Charles Percy Austin

The Mission Preservation Foundation

The Mission Preservation Foundation and organization carry out day-to-day operations and implement policy decisions based upon the following principles:

~Restoring and maintaining a sense of authenticity with regard to historic, educational, and liturgical value;

~Maintaining a "sense of peace" for all patrons of the Mission;

~Working to ensure the long-term preservation of Orange County's cultural birthplace by leveraging time and talent;

continued ➤

Festive Punch

1 gallon apple cider
2 oranges, sliced
2 lemons, sliced
5 cinnamon sticks
10 whole cloves
1 tablespoon ground allspice
2 quarts cranberry juice
2 quarts club soda

Mix the apple cider, orange slices, lemon slices, cinnamon sticks, cloves and allspice in a large saucepan and heat at just below a simmer for 40 minutes. Cool and strain into a punch bowl, discarding the fruit slices and spices. Add the cranberry juice and club soda to the punch bowl and mix gently. Add ice and garnish with fresh orange slices and lemon slices.

Serves 16

Tequila Punch

2 (46-ounce) cans unsweetened grapefruit juice, chilled
1 cup fresh lemon juice
4 cups tequila
2 (12-ounce) cans ginger ale, chilled

Combine the grapefruit juice and lemon juice with the tequila in a large refrigerator container. Chill in the refrigerator. Combine half the mixture with half the ginger ale over cracked ice in a punch bowl and mix gently. Repeat with the remaining ingredients as needed.

Serves 24 to 30

Great Stone Church Ruins, circa 2001

~Secure funding for current and future needs; utilizing modern methods of management and technology to safeguard the beauty and integrity of the Mission from intrusion and stress;

~Creating a learning environment that is inviting and attracting repeat students and visitors from all over the world to enjoy, learn, and celebrate history;

~Preserving an environment whose roots and living history continue to allow for a thriving place of pilgrimage;

~Assuring that the legacy of a unique environment is managed in a loving and steadfast manner to assure its stories remain available for all to enjoy.

The Legacy of the Mission

Looking forward, the legacy of the Mission resides in its well-established and unique position as Orange County's only mission and most historically significant site. Future efforts will focus on preservation of specific site features and upgrading existing educational programs via a well-planned museum expansion plan. The Preservation Team is focusing on much-needed museum upgrades and long-term site conservation needs to ensure The Mission's viability for generations to come.

continued ➤

Spiced Coffee

1 gallon cold water
1 1/2 cups ground coffee
1 (8-inch) cinnamon stick
2 teaspoons whole cloves

Place the water in a 30-cup electric coffee maker. Combine the ground coffee, cinnamon stick and cloves in the basket of the coffee maker. Run through a brewing cycle and serve hot or iced. Garnish iced coffee with lemon slices.

Serves 16

Hot Mulled Wine

1$\frac{1}{2}$ cups water
$\frac{1}{2}$ cup sugar
$\frac{1}{2}$ lemon, thinly sliced
3 cinnamon sticks
3 whole cloves
1 (750-milliliter) bottle red wine

Bring the water to a boil in a saucepan. Add the sugar, lemon slices, cinnamon sticks and cloves. Cook until the sugar dissolves, stirring constantly. Add the wine and reduce the heat. Simmer for 20 minutes; do not allow to boil. Strain and serve hot.

Serves 6

MSJC's historic Campanario or Mission Bell Wall reflects in a fountain.

The museum staff is working to improve the educational value of a field trip to the Mission. The team wants to ensure that the legacy of this place of peace continues and that the original building and site features remain intact for generations to come.

Bibliography

Bruton, Lydian, *The Swallows of San Juan Capistrano,* Orange, CA, The Paragon Agency, 1975.

Hallan-Gibson, Pamela, *Dos Cientos a Nos en San Juan Capistrano,* Orange, CA, The Paragon Agency, 2001.

Hallan-Gibson, Pamela, *Ghosts and Legends of San Juan Capistrano,* Pamela Hallan-Gibson, 1983.

Hallan-Gibson, Pamela, *Two Hundred Years in San Juan Capistrano, A Pictorial History,*
Orange, CA, The Paragon Agency, 2005.

Hunt, Rockwell D. and Nellie Van de Grift Sanchez, *A Short History of California,*
Thomas Y. Crowell Company, 1929.

Krammerer, Raymond C., *Old Mission San Juan Capistrano,*
Cincinnati, OH, K/M Communications, 1980.

Krekelberg, William Reverend, *Mission San Juan Capistrano,*
The Fall and Rise of a California Mission, Diocese of Orange in CA, 2004.

O'Sullivan, St. John, *Little Chapters about San Juan Capistrano,*
San Juan Capistrano, CA, St. John O'Sullivan, 1912.

Saunders, Charles Francis and Father St. John O'Sullivan, *Capistrano Nights,*
Tales of a California Mission Town, New York, Robert M. McBride & Company, 1930.

Schafer, Robert G., Coroni and Nu, *People of San Juan Capistrano Mission in the Colonial Period, 1777–1848,* San Juan Capistrano, Archive Press, 2004.

Smith, Joan Irvine and Jean Stern, *California, This Golden Land of Promise,* Irvine, CA, Chapman University Press, The Irvine Museum, 2001.

The Irvine Museum, *Romance of the Bells, The California Missions in Art,* Irvine, CA, The Irvine Museum, 1995.

Tryon, Mary Ellen, *A Guide to Historic San Juan Capistrano—Established in 1776,* Orange, CA, The Paragon Agency, 1999.

Walker, Kathleen, *Mission San Juan Capistrano, A Place of Peace,* Phoenix, AZ, Arizona Department of Transportation, 2002.

Weber, Francis J., Msgr, *The Jewel of the Missions, San Juan Capistrano,* Mission Museum Press, 1992.

Web Site Resources

www.missionsjc.com

www.sjchistoricalsociety.com

www.californiamissions.com

Mission San Juan Capistrano
Jewel of the Mission
FINANCIAL DONORS AND RECIPE DONORS

The Mission San Juan Capistrano Women's Guild expresses sincere thanks to the following for their most generous contributions in support of this project:

Diamond Friends

Fluidmaster, Inc.

Mission San Juan Women's Guild

Emerald Friends

Art and Gaye Birtcher

Cedar Creek Inn

Family Honda

Anthony and Melinda Moiso

Bruce and Johni Pittenger

Ruby Friends

Sylvia Leftwich

Sapphire Friends

El Adobe Restaurant

Sarducci's Capistrano Depot

William Lyon Homes, Inc.

Aquamarine Friends

Stephen and Peggy Beal

Merrill and Carol Clisby

Capistrano Harley-Davidson

Don and Ann Delaney

Gail S. Gibson

Marie S. Goldbach

Hirsch Pipe & Supply Company, Inc.

Rudy and Joy Horsch

Jessie Talmo

The Bells are Ringing
A CALL TO TABLE

Butterflies participate in the Annual Flower Garden and Art Show.

Contributors

The Mission San Juan Capistrano Women's Guild thanks its generous members and friends who sponsored *The Bells are Ringing — A Call to Table.*

Edward Apramian

Artifacts Council, M.S.J.C.

Stephen and Peggy Beal

Elaine Biegel

Rose Borgenight

Blanche Brooks

Joella M. Bury

California Bank and Trust

E. Wyatt Cannady

Stan and Patricia Carmichael

Judith Cassidy-MacPherson

Patricia and Richard Cole

Costco Wholesale, S.J.C.

Victor and Rose Davis

Margaret "Peggie" Devlin

Charles and Alice DiLorio

Arthur Dillemuth

Frances Dixon

Docent Society, M.S.J.C.

Dan and Diana Doll

Marta Egan

Farm to Market, S.J.C.

Michael and Denise Finch

Dorothy Gaffney

Gelson's Markets

Dr. Gail S. Gibson

Andrew Gram

Ted and Georgianna Hales

Mary Jane and Jack Higgins

Frank and Dorothy Hollibaugh

Judith Hoon

Beverly Hughes

Marie Callender's Restaurant
   and Bakery, S.J.C.

Maurice and Marcia Imonti

Jon's Fish Market, Dana Point

Robert and Mary Elizabeth Kaiser

Angelina and Robert Karlson

Samir and Suad Khalaf

Living History, M.S.J.C.

Carol and Robert Lowe

Jolene Lucci

Marbella Farmer's Market, S.J.C.

Marshall's Department Store, S.J.C.

Marie McConnell

F. W. and Marjorie McGehee

John and Betty Miller

Lynn Miller

The Gardening Angels, M.S.J.C.

Gary Thornberg, *Mission Winery*

Murphy Goode Winery, Geyserville, CA

Eileen Perkett

Ralph's Market, S.J.C.

Al and Gloria Ravera

Charles and Hazel Schwab

Jim and Laura Seiler

Marilyn Silverman

Ed and Mary Smith

C. E. and Jean Spearman

Toni Sullivan

Trader Joe's Market, Laguna Niguel

Louise Truxaw

Von's Market, M.S.J.C.

Robert and Carol Westervett

Gary and Laurie Wilfert

The Bells are Ringing
A CALL TO TABLE

Recipe Contributors

Jill Badiaves

Peggy Beal

Rose Borgenight

Blanche Brooks

Joella M. Bury

Stan and Patricia Carmichael

Janet Carter

Caroline Cazaumayou

Cedar Creek Inn

Patricia Cole

Rhoda Davies

Diana Doll

Beverly Ducey

El Adobe Restaurant

El Niguel Country Club

Tony Forster

Barbara Gershman

Vivian Gormly

Very Reverend Arthur A. Holquin

Joy Horsch

Beverly Hughes

Maurice and Marcia Imonti

Lisa Inman

Liz Issac

Fabiola Johns

Angelina Karlson

Carol Lowe

Sharon Markowitz

The Late Monsignor Paul Martin

Marie McConnell

Betty Miller

Lynn Miller

Kathy O'Connell

Eugenie Oyharzabol

Eileen Perkett

Nina Perkl

Rebecca Pittinger

Gloria Ravera

Dolores Rosenberg

Mary Sand

Sarducci's Capistrano Depot

Pamela Schuler

Hazel Schwab

Marilyn Silverman

Lucinda Sire

Mary Smith

Jean Spizzirri

Steve Stevenson

Sherry Swanson

Don and Mary Tryon

Mattie Rosannan Waters

Rosalie Weigle

Phyllis Weiner

Fiona Wong

Any errors or omissions to this list are regretted.

The Bells are Ringing
A CALL TO TABLE

Cookbook Committee

Mary Smith, *Chairman*

Johni Pittenger, *Co-Chairman and History Research*

Joy Horsch, *Food Chairman*

Carol Lowe, *Recording Secretary and Recipes*

Carol Clisby, *Recipes*

Joella Bury, *Marketing*

Peggy Beal

Mary Jane Higgins

Marcia Imonti

Annabelle Isky

Mary Elizabeth Kaiser

Eileen Perkett

Dolores Rosenberg

Laura Seiler

Lucinda Sire

Toni Sullivan

Special Thanks to:

Merrill Clisby, *Financial Advisor*

Jack Higgins, *Consultant*

Mozelle Redman Sukut, Ph.D.,

   Archive Committee Research

Bev Smith, *Photography*

Lee and Sue Goode, *Living History Photography*

Ron Bauer, *Living History*

Charles L. Heizman, *Living History*

Jerry Nieblas, *Artifacts Coordinator*

Jacque Nuñez, *"Journeys to the Past"*

Jan Sorenson, *Gardening Angels*

Jessica Pittenger, *History*

Jeanna Smith-Morris, *Photo Shoot*

Marcia Equils, *Equils Advertising*

The Bells are Ringing
A CALL TO TABLE

Photograph and Artwork Index

The Bells are Ringing
A CALL TO TABLE

Index

The Bells are Ringing
A CALL TO TABLE

The Bells are Ringing
A CALL TO TABLE

The Bells are Ringing
A CALL TO TABLE

The Bells are Ringing
A CALL TO TABLE

The Bells are Ringing
A CALL TO TABLE

About Mission San Juan Capistrano

The Bells are Ringing

A CALL TO TABLE

Mission San Juan Capistrano—Cookbook Orders
26801 Ortega Highway
San Juan Capistrano, California 92675

Sales information is available on the official Mission San Juan Capistrano Web site
at www.missionsjc.com

Name of Person Placing Order

Delivery Street Address

City   State   Zip

Telephone   (daytime)   (evening)

YOUR ORDER	QUANTITY	TOTAL
The Bells are Ringing at $30.00 per book		$
California residents add $2.25 sales tax		$
Shipping and handling at $6.00 per book		$
	TOTAL	$

Method of Payment: [   ] MasterCard   [   ] Visa
                       [   ] Check enclosed payable to Mission San Juan Capistrano

Credit Card Number   Expiration Date

Signature

Photocopies and faxes: (949) 429-7834 will be accepted.

When the Swallows Come Back to Capistrano

By LEON RENÉ